THE  HANDBOOK

THE AIRFIX HANDBOOK

JAMES MAY'S
TOY STORIES

CONWAY

Acknowledgements

James May thanks the following for their help with his Airfix adventures, with the research for the text and sourcing the illustrations.

Anova Books, in particular Ian Harrison, Polly Powell, John Lee, Matthew Jones, Fiona Holman, Alison Moss, Georgina Hewitt, Nichola Smith, Laura Brodie and Oliver Jeffreys.
Plum Pictures, in particular Vicki Bax, Abi Brooks, Paul Buller, Stuart Cabb, Will Daws, Alex Dunlop, Jules Endersby, Ian Holt, Charlie Hyland, Nick Kennedy, Rebecca Magill, David Marks, Sim Oakley, Martin Phillip, Lareine Shea, Warren Smith, Graham Strong and Becky Timothy.
Also **Component Graphics** for the logo design, TV title sequence, book jacket graphics and programme graphics; Caroline Allen, Simon Rogers and Michael Wicks.
Airfix®, especially the inventor of Airfix, Nicholas Kove; also Poppy Boden (Cast For Life: www.castforlife.co.uk); Darrell Burge, Dale Luckhurst and all at Hornby Hobbies Ltd (www.hornby.com); Alex Medhurst and all the staff at RAF Cosford; Jonathan Mock; Roy Cross; Chris Ellis; Gateguards (www.gateguardsuk.com); Carolyn Grace (www.ml407.co.uk); James May Sr. (James's dad); Trevor Snowden; Arthur Ward and Ebury Press; Ken Wilkinson; and the staff, pupils and their parents from Thomas Telford School.

First published in the United Kingdom in 2010 by Conway,
an imprint of Anova Books,
10 Southcombe Street
London W14 0RA

Produced in association with Plum Pictures Limited,
33 Oval Road, London NW1 7EA

British Library Cataloguing in Publication Data:
A catalogue record for this book is available from the British Library.

10 9 8 7 6 5 4 3 2

ISBN 9781844861163

Distributed in the U.S. and Canada by:
Sterling Publishing Co., Inc.
387 Park Avenue South
New York, NY 10016-8810

Reproduction by Rival Colour Ltd.
Printed and bound by 1010 Printing International Ltd, China.

www.anovabooks.com
www.conwaypublishing.com

CONTENTS

Why Airfix?

For me, Airfix is, without doubt, the ultimate boys' toy. The first thing I proposed for the *Toy Stories* series was to build an Airfix model the size of a real aeroplane, because that's what I'd always imagined doing as a child. And it had to be a Spitfire because – apart from its iconic status as a symbol of the best of British – the Spitfire was the first plane that Airfix modelled and it is still the best-selling Airfix kit of all time.

The Spitfire was also my first Airfix model. I'm not quite old enough to remember Airfix's very first Spitfire, the Mk I (BTK), because that went out of production very quickly, but I did have the Mk IX, which was first released in 1955 and remained in production for some time. I can still remember being given it. When I was about five years old we were staying in a little seaside town and I

"Kit construction is part of the male life cycle."

remember going into a small corner shop and seeing these intriguing looking toys hanging on hooks in the now-famous poly bags. I'd never seen an Airfix model so I picked one up and said to my dad, 'What's this?'

I wasn't being totally stupid – it was a model tank, so the bag was full of very small bits and it wasn't really clear what it was. There was a picture of a tank on the header but my five-year-old self certainly couldn't see a tank in the bag. My dad told me it was an Airfix model and when I asked if I could try making one he said, 'Yes, but don't do that one because that's really fiddly.' And he took it off me and put it back on the hook. Then he took down the Spitfire and said, 'Do this, you'll like this one more.'

How right he was.

I don't think my dad had ever made an Airfix kit because he was from the era when you made models by hand-carving bits of wood. But he

knew what Airfix was and he was pretty keen to have a go at it too. And that was the thing. It may have been made out of new-fangled plastic, and it may not have involved carving the pieces by hand, but Dad could approve of it because it was still a toy that tested your practical skills and exercised your imagination. As Airfix historian Arthur Ward puts it, kit construction is 'a truly interactive hobby. Airfix supply the raw materials and all [you] have to do is bring a modicum of ability, some patience and abundant imagination. The result is always something to be proud of.'

Well, almost always.

But for some reason kit construction engages boys' imaginations more than girls' – and that's not just me being prejudiced, it's a fact borne out by Airfix's sales figures and by my own experience. My girlfriend remembers being terribly disappointed with Airfix because there was a fantastic picture on the box but when she took off the lid all she found was some crumpled bits of plastic. But for boys that's not the point – the picture means that when you start making the model you're in that scene; it isn't little bits of plastic, it's a real aeroplane and you're flying it and there really are bandits at three o'clock trying to shoot you down. And that's something no computer game can do: in a computer game you're tied to the imagination of the programmer but with Airfix the artist's imagination is a springboard for your own.

And as well as firing the imagination there was also the educational aspect. The whole point of making models when I was a kid was that they were supposed to be educational. Not modern, high-falutin', theoretical,

hand-eye co-ordination type education. Real education – learning facts about things you wouldn't other-wise have found out about. Airfix was obsessed with historical details and thought everybody else should be too, so all the instruction leaflets had snippets of information or a potted history of whatever you were making.

You might think that as a child the idea that I was educating myself would have put me off, but it didn't. There were always unfinished Airfix models lying around our house because I would get involved with making several at the same time. It was youthful exuberance, excitement, and impatience to make a start on the next kit, and my friends were the same. So the big question is: why aren't 13-year-olds today as excited about Airfix as I was and all my mates were when we were 13? Airfix sales are still high but its market has changed since I was a child: a large proportion of buyers are men in their 40s, like me.

Darrell Burge, Airfix's marketing manager, told me that Airfix is considering developing a simplified range because while adult modellers are demanding more and more detail children are coping with fewer and fewer parts – not because they're less skilful than they used to be but because there are so many other activities competing for their time. Thankfully Airfix is not dumbing down completely. There are no plans for ready-painted, clip-together kits, so there is a place for glue and paint in the future of Airfix. And at least when the simplified range appears there will still be proper kits for those of us who want to relive our lost youth by recreating the glories of the ultimate boys' toy.

Remember: you don't have to grow up. Kit construction is part of the male life cycle. When you reach a certain age you retire to the shed and you return to Airfix. Shakespeare got it wrong with his seven ages of man. Really there are three – Airfix, Adulthood, and Airfix Revisited.

From combs to kits

The name Airfix is almost synonymous with scale model aircraft. The two are so closely related that it's tempting to think Airfix invented the plastic construction kit and that the company was named after the concept.

In fact, neither is true. And Airfix's first kit wasn't even a plane.

The first plastic scale model aircraft kits were marketed by Frog in 1936, a full 17 years before Airfix produced its first kit plane (a Spitfire Mk I). And the name derives from the fact that the company originally made air-filled rubber toys. Founder Nicholas Kove wanted a name beginning with 'A' because he thought it would help his fledgling business if it had a name that would appear near the front of trade directories. 'Air' was the obvious A-word because that's what his products were filled with, and he thought that names ending in '-ix' sounded distinctive. So he put the two together and one of the most legendary names in the toy industry was born – but it didn't make construction kits.

Kove was interested in synthetic materials, and he founded Airfix in 1939 to exploit the market for air-filled rubber toys such as squeezable rubber building bricks. When supplies of latex were curtailed during World War II the inventive and determined Kove simply moved from

Below: The Ferguson tractor, which was arguably the first kit to be produced by Airfix. However, the first version of this legendary tractor was not a construction kit but a ready-assembled promotional item made at the request of Harry Ferguson so that his sales reps could demonstrate the key features of the tractor.

Above: 1990s box art: four decades after its first release the *Golden Hind* was still in the Airfix range, now packaged in a box rather than a bag.

rubber to plastics. Airfix's first successful plastic product was a utility lighter; then came Airfix baby rattles, and then the product that is the true precursor of the kits we know today – plastic combs. By 1947 Airfix was the biggest manufacturer of plastic combs in Britain. But what is more historically significant than the product, or the volume sold, was the production method. The traditional way to make plastic combs was to cut them out of a solid piece of acetate. Kove could see this was wasteful and time-consuming, so he invested in what was then a very modern piece of machinery: an injection-moulding machine.

Injection moulding enabled Kove to mass-produce combs very cheaply, and it is still the method by which Airfix kits are made today. However, Airfix is now a little more discerning about its raw materials and its finish. Immediately after the war plastics were still rationed so Kove fed his machines with whatever scrap materials were available, ranging (or so the story goes) from unwanted acetate fountain pens to the rubber casing of electrical cables. Kove was even shrewd enough to keep his raw materials uniformly poor, and when he did manage to get hold of first-grade raw materials he would mix them with second-grade plastics so that his customers weren't spoilt when circumstances forced him to revert to purely second-grade materials.

Airfix celebrated its 60th anniversary in 2009 but this date is somewhat confusing. The company was founded in 1939, 70 years earlier, and first mass-marketed a construction kit in 1952, 57 years earlier.

The reason the anniversary dates from 1949 is that that was the year when Airfix produced what was arguably its first kit – a 1:20 scale replica of a Ferguson tractor. The first version of the tractor was a ready-assembled promotional item but the following year Airfix began supplying the tractor to Ferguson as a 40-part construction kit. However, this was for practical reasons rather than being a conscious move towards the production of kits. Ralph Ehrmann, a former Chairman of Airfix Industries, later recalled: '[We] decided that because the assembled tractor was so fiddly and regularly fell to bits it was perhaps a good idea to actually sell it as a kit of parts and let someone else have the headache of assembling it!' Later still, Airfix decided to sell the kit to the general public and Ferguson, of course, was only too pleased to give its consent to this free publicity.

But the story of Airfix construction kits really begins in 1952 with the *Golden Hind*.

Below: The *Golden Hind* and I IMS *Shannon*, two of the first three ships in the Airfix Historic Ships range. Eight ships of the Royal Navy have been called *Shannon*. The most famous was this frigate, which fought an epic battle with the US frigate *Chesapeake* during the War of 1812, which was the last war (to date!) to be fought between Britain and the US.

The *Golden Hind* and the Woolworths connection

The *Golden Hind* has several claims to being Airfix's first true construction kit: it was the first to be conceived from the outset as a construction kit; the first kit to be produced specifically for retail sale; the first to be moulded in polystyrene (the tractor had been moulded in acetate, which is one of the reasons pieces often dropped off); and, perhaps most important, the first to be sold in the iconic 'poly bag' – a form of packaging which was phased out in 1973, to make way for modern 'blister packs', but reintroduced in 2000. As with the supply of the tractor as a kit, the genesis of the poly bag was more serendipitous than planned. It arose because of a dispute with Woolworths over pricing of the kit.

The economic advantages of retailing construction kits were not lost on the managers of Airfix after their experience with the Ferguson tractor: instead of having to pay staff to assemble and paint a finished model, all that was required, to quote Airfix historian Arthur Ward, 'was to insert the moulded frames directly into a box with the addition of a cheap one-colour instruction sheet and some crude decals to boot.'

But Airfix's premier retailer, Woolworths, had made a similar calculation and refused to retail a box of unassembled parts at the same price as they had the assembled tractor. The only way that Airfix could meet the lower price point was to package the kit not in a box but in a polythene bag, with a folded header carrying an illustration of the finished kit on the outside and the instructions on the inside. Like many great ideas, this one was born of necessity and it went on to become an institution. Many are the collectors who recall taking their pocket money to Woolworths as children and seeing the familiar array of poly bags hanging on the display stand containing the wherewithal for a journey to polystyrene wonderland.

The response to the *Golden Hind* and the other bagged kits which soon followed was phenomenal. Airfix had worried about its margins at the low price point stipulated by Woolworths but it needn't have done. Ehrmann remembers that production runs of the kits were soon in the order of hundreds of thousands rather than the expected tens of thousands; polythene bags were coming down in price; polystyrene dropped in price by

Above: Box art for the 'Dogfight Doubles' kit of the Spitfire Mk IX and the Messerschmitt Bf110, 1975.

about two thirds, and as production became ever more efficient Airfix was making 30 per cent profit on each item.

The choice of the *Golden Hind* was reputedly that of the Woolworths buyer, who suggested it because a ship-in-a-bottle version was selling well in the US. Its success was immediate and over the next few years Airfix produced several other sailing ships to create a Historical Ships range, which was sold both as individual kits and as a boxed set known as the Airfix Armada. The *Golden Hind* has remained in the Airfix range almost ever since, and a new 1:72 scale model of 109 pieces appears in the 60th anniversary catalogue.

Meanwhile, Airfix continued to produce other 'pocket-money toys' but the success of the construction kits had been so great that the company naturally focussed on kits as its core product. Legend has it that Kove was so pleased with sales of the Historical Ships range that he saw no need to diversify into kits of aircraft or vehicles. However, it appears that either this isn't true or his senior managers ignored him – the only kit to be introduced in 1953 (the year after the *Golden Hind*) was an aircraft: the Spitfire Mk I. The following year saw the release of two ships (*Santa Maria* and *Shannon*) and 1955 saw two more ships, a second aircraft (a Spitfire Mk IX) and Airfix's first vehicle (a 1911 Rolls Royce). By 1956 aircraft were already in the majority: by then Airfix had produced eight aircraft, seven ships and six cars.

It was a pattern that would continue. Aircraft soon became the staple of Airfix kits and the area in which the company was to become most famous worldwide – possibly, in part, because the name of the brand gives the impression that aircraft are its core product. In 2009 aircraft dominate the range, accounting for 60 per cent of all Airfix kits. But, as current marketing manager Darrell Burge points out, that still leaves 40 per cent for other areas. 'In fact,' he says, 'if you look just at the smaller kits at the lower price points, tanks sell better overall than aircraft of the same price.' And the 60th anniversary catalogue further dispels the myth that Airfix is all about aircraft, asserting merely that: 'One of the most important parts of the Airfix range is the aircraft category.'

Below: Airfix's diverse range includes many modern and historical military aircraft, vehicles and figures, from First World War biplanes to German paratroops.

Kits in context

To understand the impact that Airfix kits had on modelling it is necessary to consider them in the context of toys at the time. At the beginning of the 20th century model-making still meant creating your own models from scratch. Enthusiasts needed an aptitude for woodwork or metalwork or both, and often owned equipment unlikely to be found in the average household today: soldering irons, brazing irons, lathes, and all manner of woodworking tools, which were used to convert raw materials (sheet metal or blocks of wood) into working models. By the end of the 19th century model railway companies had begun producing metal construction kits of locomotives, and later aircraft modelling companies such as the aptly named Aeromodels began producing kits with partially formed components which modellers had to shape themselves before assembling the kits.

The first aircraft construction kit made up of fully finished components was a Cierva C24 Autogyro, marketed in the 1930s by the British company Sky Birds. It was also the first to be scaled at 1:72, which became a standard scale and remains the most popular scale in the Airfix range to this day. Producing a kit of finished components proved to be a

Below: British manufacturer Sky Birds was the first to produce a kit comprising fully finished components. Sky Birds also pioneered the 1:72 scale, which to this day remains the most popular scale in the Airfix range.

popular innovation – there was a wide market among those who did not have the time, the equipment, the space or the skills required for traditional model engineering – and by 1935 Sky Birds boasted a range of 20 models.

However, in 1936 Sky Birds was beaten to a more significant first. That Christmas another British company, Frog, released the first scale model construction kit to be made entirely from plastic. Frog, which was already renowned for its flying scale models, named its new range of non-flying, detailed plastic replicas the 'Penguin series' – Penguins being a bird that cannot fly. After the war Frog extended its range to include vehicles and ships, making the Penguin series arguably the true precursor of all modern plastic scale model construction kits.

However, there is one considerable difference between the early Frog kits and their modern descendants: the plastic they are made from. Frog kits were made from a very early thermoplastic known as cellulose acetate butyrate, which often warped and did not age well. After the war, when research and development in plastics were no longer restricted to the war effort, materials improved quickly. Airfix's Ferguson tractor was made of acetate but the *Golden Hind*, released just three years later, was moulded from a far superior plastic: polystyrene. Ralph Ehrmann is in no doubt that Airfix's early adoption of polystyrene was key to its success, telling Airfix historian Arthur Ward: 'There were models on the British market before *Golden Hind* but they were always in acetate, which was hydrotropic and always twisted so that you couldn't make a decent model from it. The fact that polystyrene came onto the market made a lot of difference.'

Left: Exhibitors arrive for the Model Engineer and Aircraft Exhibition at the New Horticultural Hall in Westminster on 19 August 1958. Peter Blanshot cycled to the exhibition from Chiswick with his model of a Staysail Schooner on a trailer. Colin and Leslie Smith, ten and eight, are carrying their father's models of the Fairey Delta II and Deltaceptor.
Below: By Christmas 1936 the British company, Frog, released the first scale model construction kits to be made entirely from plastic.

From the drawing board to the display stand

Today, the injection moulding of polystyrene is still the key part of producing Airfix kits but it is only one part of a long drawn-out process – it can take over a year between deciding to go ahead with a model and that model reaching the shops.

The first step is to design the model, which can take several months. Before the days of computers the designers would execute a series of drawings based either on manufacturer's drawings or on their own measurements, starting with a 'general arrangement' and then moving to a scale drawing which would be broken down into individual components, each of which required a separate set of working drawings. Interestingly, even in the computer age, designing the components is not simply a question of scaling down the originals. Some details are too fine to mould (the molten plastic would simply not reach those extremities of the mould) or too fragile once moulded, and others would look wrong even though they were correct. For instance, the designer of the Airfix Mini revealed that the door handles were 'cheated' because if he had scaled them accurately they would have been 'just a thin wisp' and have looked wrong. 'Your designer's eye allowed you to strike a balance.'

Below: An Airfix Spitfire mould. The propeller, tail planes and pilot figure can clearly be seen, carved in relief into the metal block.

Once the design is completed (whether by computer or by hand), creating the moulding tool can take several more months: this involves cutting the shape of each component into two halves of a mould which, when locked together, leave a kit-shaped gap that will be filled with molten plastic. Only then, when the tools are ready and tested, can the injection-moulding process begin, at which point a torrent of newly moulded kits begins pouring off the production line for packing and distribution. Meanwhile, myriad other pieces of the puzzle must have been completed, such as designing the artwork for the packaging, photographing the model for the catalogue and so on.

But at the heart of the whole process is the injection moulding itself. Polystyrene is a 'thermoplastic', which means it is liquid when heated but completely rigid when cool; thus it can be heated up, injected into a mould and, once cooled, it retains the shape of the mould. Modern thermoplastics replicate the tiniest detail of the finely tooled moulds, which means that 21st-century models can be intricately detailed to a degree that early designers could only have dreamt of, right down to rivets and screwheads at true scale size. The moulds are water-cooled to keep them below the setting temperature of the plastic, which means that once the injection has taken place the plastic sets almost instantly. The mould, which is in two parts, is then opened and the finished article is ejected by a set of 'ejector pins' that push it out of the casing. With early injection-moulding machines the ejector pins would often leave tell-tale circular marks where the plastic had not fully set, but with modern methods this is now a rare occurrence.

Injection, setting and ejection of the plastic takes about 30 seconds, which means that one machine can spew out more than 100 kits an hour. Modellers may not think it very romantic that the kit they spend hours lovingly assembling has been disgorged so rapidly and mechanically from the mould, but they can console themselves with the thought that the real skill and attention to detail has been put in with equally loving care by the designers much earlier in the process.

Overleaf: Original technical drawings from Supermarine's owners Vickers-Armstrong showing the general arrangement of the Spitfire Mk V. Airfix's 1:48 kit version is shown right.

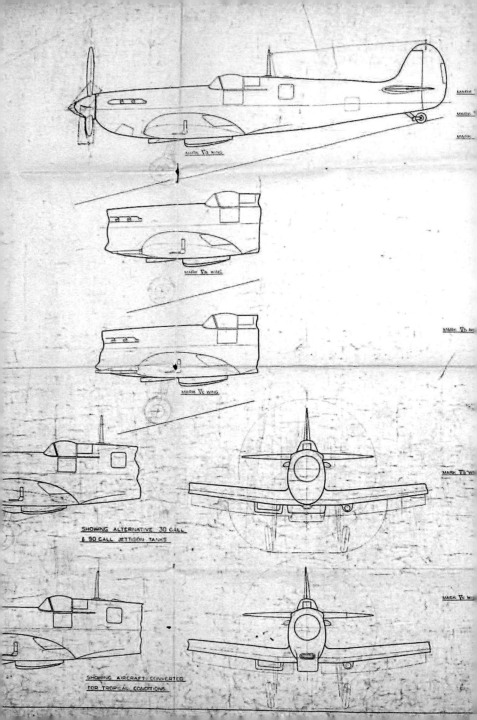

MARK I

MARK

MARK

MARK I WING

MARK Vb WING

MARK Vb WING

MARK Vc WING

MARK Vb WING

SHOWING ALTERNATIVE 30 GALL
& 90 GALL JETTISON TANKS

MARK Vc WING

SHOWING AIRCRAFT CONVERTED
FOR TROPICAL CONDITIONS

MARK VI WING

MARK Vb WING

MARK Vc WING

MARK V

MARK Vb

MARK Vc

GENERAL

ROLL

Common faults

Model kits have come a long way since I was a lad, and the blobby little pilots that I remember from childhood seem to have given way to chiselled, steely-eyed airmen. Still, plastic injection moulding isn't an exact science, and all models supplied in kit form generally require a bit of cleaning up before you get 'stuck in' (literally, in some cases). Here are some common faults to look out for – take care of these and you'll be well on the way to making a model that you can be truly proud of. Understanding what a 'sink mark' is will also demystify lots of strange modelling talk you might hear going on in model shops or at conventions – and if you join in with such conversations it'll make you sound like a pro. In the case of 'flashing' it might also save a lot of embarrassment.

Know your modelling terms

Sprues, gates and runners – what's the difference?

Although most modellers generally refer only to 'sprues' and 'parts', technically there is a distinction between sprues, gates and runners, all of which are important in the injection moulding process. The 'gate' is the location at which the molten plastic is injected into the mould, and is often seen as a small stubby projection (a 'gate mark' or 'injector stub') on the outside edge of a moulded piece. The 'runners' are the large-

diameter channels through which plastic flows, usually around the edges of the part or along straight lines. So the term 'sprue' refers only to the smaller channels that lead from the runners to the individual part – they're the bits of plastic you have to cut or snap off to remove the pieces of a kit. So now you know...

1 **Ejector pin mark:** Ejector pins are small cylindrical rods that form a key part of the machines used in the injection moulding process. They lie flush with the mould during casting (i.e. when the molten plastic is injected), but pop out once the process is complete in order to push the newly formed kit out of its mould. A good thing – this means each machine can produce more than 100 kits an hour. If the plastic hasn't set hard enough

before it is pushed out of the mould, the ejector pin often leaves a small but telltale circular mark on the kit. Although less common than they used to be, most kits will have at least one or two pin marks. They are actually less of a problem on cheaper kits, as most parts only have detail on one side, so the manufacturers sensibly place the pin locations on the unmoulded half, where a mark won't be such an issue (e.g. on the inside of an aircraft fuselage). But with higher-spec kits it is virtually impossible to avoid a pin mark on a detailed area. The application of a little modelling filler or putty will usually sort these out.

2 **Sink mark:** This is basically a depression in the surface of the plastic kit, usually caused because insufficient plastic has been injected to fill a particular part of the mould, or if there was not enough pressure to fully push the molten plastic into the cavity. As a result, they usually appear towards the middle of a sprue or on a particularly thick part of the kit. Again some trusty filler can be applied and shaped to create a smooth finish.

3 **Flashing:** This is a thin web or fin of plastic that protrudes from the edge of a plastic part. They are also often found around delicate bits of a kit, and are caused by some excess plastic leaking into the space between the two halves of a mould – working and operating clearances means that the fit of these is rarely perfect. However, some careful trimming with a craft knife (watch those fingers!) will solve the problem, and will really improve the details of the finished kit.

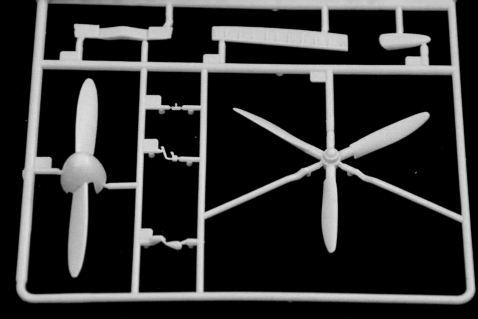

4 **Injector stubs or gate marks** Fairly rare, and usually only found in more expensive limited-run kits (due to the lower pressure used in moulding), injector stubs are the points where excess plastic is extruded from the mould. They can be removed with a knife or sanded off.

5 **Checking:** Checking is the name given to the series of thin lines or raised veins occasionally visible on the surface of a plastic part. Usually found on vintage kits produced from old moulds or kits from the end of a long production run, they are the impression of fine cracks on the surface of the moulds caused by the wear and tear that comes about from repeated exposure to hot plastic. Lightly sanding the relevant part should help reduce the visibility of checking.

6 **Knit line:** This is the wavy line seen on the larger pieces of a plastic kit. During production molten plastic is injected into the mould at different points ('gates'), shooting through all the gaps to meet in the middle and create a complete sprue. If the plastic has already partially cooled, different surface textures develop and when the plastic originating from two different injection points meets, a knit line is formed. They do not alter the integrity of the part itself other than how it looks. So although a wavy line and perhaps some colour variation will be visible in the plastic, don't worry – once painted you won't be able to tell.

7 Draft angle: Not a fault in itself, but a piece of technical jargon that explains why some pieces of a kit often seem to be better moulded than others, particularly in terms of surface detail. It helps to remember that the moulds used for making plastic kits are essentially large, flat metal plates. The details of the model are carved into the surface of this plate in relief. Carving straight into the mould produces a surface that is parallel to the flat plane of the mould. Detail carved in this way will be crisp and clean. This becomes obvious when you lay a sprue flat on a table and look directly down at it. However, it is far more difficult to carve detail sideways into a mould plate. Pick the sprue up and look at it along an edge. You'll notice that the details start to soften the further away the plastic surface is from the parallel plane of the sprue. Designers have to work with such limitations – and so a draft angle is incorporated into a wall of a mould. This enables the plastic part to be ejected easily, otherwise the sprue, which contracts as it cools, would 'stick' to the metal mould.

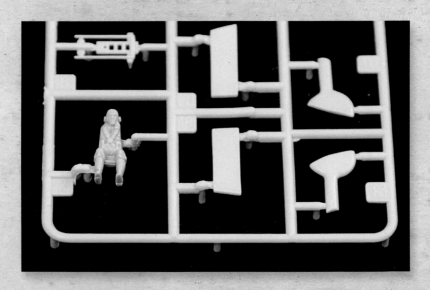

The doyen of Airfix artists

In my opinion Roy Cross is the most influential British artist of the 20th century. He must be, given the number of 1960s and 1970s schoolboys who saw his artwork on the Airfix boxes and thought, 'That's what I want for my birthday' – the number of imaginations he fired to believe that, rather than zooming a little plastic model round their bedrooms at arm's length, they were actually flying the real thing. But Roy, who is now in his 80s, is too modest to accept that, telling me: 'Let's just say I'm one of the most exposed.'

I visited Roy at home to persuade him to sketch the artwork for my giant kit. He told me that in his day he would use test mouldings of the new models as maquettes so that he could hold the model at various angles to find the one that would look best in what he called 'that stupid letterbox' – the wide, shallow shape of the Airfix box top. I tried the same thing with a model Spitfire and settled on a view of the underside of the plane as it climbed away from the onlooker. Roy sketched that viewpoint in double quick time and I then had his sketch computer-rendered into the artwork for my 1:1 scale Spitfire. The computer-generated artwork was perfect for the model but I still treasure my original Roy Cross sketch.

Left: Original action-packed box art for the Boeing B-1/G Flying Fortress (1962). There's a lot going on.

Right: Roy and I discuss artwork for the 1:1 scale Spitfire (2009).

Below: Classic Roy Cross artwork on the packaging of the Blenheim IV (1968) and the Wellington B.III (1958).

Bottom: The signed sketch that was used to create the box art for my BTK, showing my preferred view of the underside of the plane.

A selection of evocative Roy Cross artworks, all of which adorned the boxes of Airfix kits for many years. Clockwise, from top left: a Japanese Aichi D3A1 Val dive-bomber climbs away from a U.S. aircraft carrier; an RAF Lancaster bomber comes in to land, badly shot up and with its port engine ablaze; an American B-26 Marauder medium bomber dropping its payload; and a yellow-nosed Messerschmitt Bf109, perhaps the Luftwaffe's most famous fighter, and traditional adversary of the Spitfire.

Spitfire BTK

Although the moulding machines and the plastics have improved since 1952, all Airfix kits are made by basically the same process as the first two models: the *Golden Hind* and the Spitfire Mk I. It seems appropriate that the first aircraft construction kit to be produced by such a great British company should be such a great British icon, but in fact it seems that the Airfix model was copied from a model manufactured by the American company Aurora. Former Airfix MD John Grey told Arthur Ward that the 1:48 scale Aurora kit was copied at a reduced scale of 1:72 to produce a mould for the Airfix version, but whether this was done by agreement with Aurora or not is unclear. What is clear is that the Airfix model was copied so faithfully that it replicated a number of significant errors in the Aurora model.

The Airfix kit, which had 21 parts in blue plastic, was released in 1953 and sold in huge numbers. However, this commercial triumph was offset by critical disaster as letters flooded in from modellers and former RAF fitters complaining about errors in the profile, the wing shape, the dimensions and other details of the aircraft. The most obvious error of all, also carried over from the Aurora to the Airfix model, was the squadron code BTK. This had never appeared on a Spitfire but was actually a code used by a Supermarine Walrus squadron, the Walrus being an amphibious

Below: The very first Airfix aircraft construction kit, the Spitfire Mk I 'BTK'. On the left is the 2010 reissue, still poly-bagged, but a much improved version complete with *Toy Stories* artwork on the header card.

Above: Current box artwork for the 1:24 scale Spitfire Mk IA 'Super Kit', which 'took the modelling world by storm' when it was first released in 1970. The kit has been in production ever since.

biplane. This error has become the stuff of toy-making legend (like Action Man's inverted thumbnail), and although the error-ridden model was soon replaced in the Airfix range it remains important to collectors. The error was celebrated again during Airfix's 60th anniversary when the code BTK was chosen for the largest ever kit to be constructed on the Airfix principle: the 1:1 scale Spitfire Mk I built at RAF Cosford in 2009.

One of the many modellers to complain about the inaccuracies of the Airfix Mk I was John Edwards, who told Airfix that he could do better himself. Edwards duly became their chief designer and in 1955 he proved that his faith in his own abilities was well founded – Airfix released its second aircraft kit, a much more accurate Spitfire Mk IX, which was so popular that it remained in the Airfix range for more than 40 years (having been remoulded in 1960) and was still present in the 50th anniversary catalogue of 1999. And so, partially due to the inaccuracies of its first Spitfire, Airfix gained a chief designer who was to remain with the company for 15 years (until his early death at the age of 38) and who would become famous throughout the modelling industry for the quality and accuracy of his designs.

One of Edwards' last projects was another Spitfire, the renowned 1:24

scale Spitfire Mk IA, which was released in 1970. This kit – the first in a new range of 'Super Kits' – took kit manufacturing to new heights, and even included a 1.5 volt 'Propmotor' to power the propeller. Arthur Ward is in no doubt as to its significance: 'It took the modelling world by storm. Almost overnight Airfix had set new standards and most of their competitors were left far behind… When the new Spitfire appeared, with its 18-inch wingspan, cockpit, engine and even wing gun-bay detail, modellers rushed to the shops to see how the kit went together.' The Spitfire has remained a perennially popular subject ever since, and in all Airfix has produced 22 different versions including the five kits scheduled for release in 2010.

Until his untimely death, Edwards directed the design of all Airfix kits, not just aircraft, in a range that rapidly broadened from ships, planes and cars to include: model railway accessories (1957 onwards); 1:12 scale historical figures (1959 onwards); railway rolling stock (1959 onwards); military vehicles (1961 onwards), and licensed character models, starting in 1965 with the James Bond and Oddjob diorama. Airfix was on a seemingly unstoppable escalator, constantly improving its range, its quality and its profit margins. At this stage no one could have predicted that before the company's 60th anniversary it would have gone bust – twice.

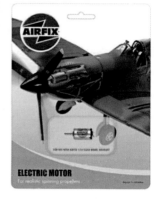

Right: Airfix's 1:24 Spitfire kit features a detailed engine bay, which can be modelled with the cowling removed to display the intricate parts. The engine parts can also be built around the electric prop-motor above, which enables the propeller to spin realistically. Unfortunately it doesn't recreate the signature roar of the Rolls-Royce Merlin engine.

Spitfire kits

The Spitfire is the world's most popular model aircraft kit. There must be millions of Spitfire models out there – even Airfix have produced a remarkable 22 different kits.

1 **1:72 Spitfire BTK (1953)** The original Spit kit from 1953, and the basis for my 1:1 scale model. Copied from a US-manufactured Aurora kit in 1:48 scale, it supposedly represents a Mk I (although this isn't certain) but has various inaccuracies. For example, the kit includes four small bombs, two under each wing. The real Spitfire only ever carried one bomb under each wing. The landing gear is also moulded into the wings, so that if the extended landing gear is glued in place, the plane has the gear both stowed and deployed at the same time! The decals supplied were also incorrect – in fact, the serial number 'BTK' was never used by an RAF Spitfire. But despite these errors, we should all be truly thankful for this kit. It paved the way for all of Airfix's subsequent range of scale model aircraft, and gave hours of fun to post-war children – for the modest price of two shillings. Today, an original BTK model will set you back between £100 and £150. If you want to build it, Airfix have re-released a retro blue plastic version for 2010, complete with poly-bag and header card.

2 **1:72 Spitfire Mk IX (1955, re-released in 1960)** Johnnie Johnson's JE-J machine was Airfix's first attempt to tool a more accurate Spitfire. Designer John Edwards improved the mould after he had become better acquainted with the intricacies of plastic injection moulding. A fondly remembered kit, which for many dads evokes great nostalgia as the first Airfix kit they ever built.

3 **1:24 Supermarine Spitfire Mk I (1970)** This ambitious undertaking was Airfix's first kit in this scale, and was in fact the first 1:24 scale model kit to be produced by any manufacturer in the world. Airfix branded the model a 'super kit', and not without some justification – the finished model has a wingspan of over 18 inches and is more than 14 inches long. Various detailed parts were provided: removable wing panels enabled the .30 Browning machine guns to be displayed, similarly removable engine panels showcased the Rolls-Royce Merlin engine, and the canopy could be modelled in its open position to show the cockpit interior, with instrument panels, flight controls, seat harness and other features. For the time this demonstrated a sensational attention to detail.

4 **1:72 Spitfire Mk Vb (1974)** Airfix's third Spitfire in this scale represented the MkV, which was produced in greater numbers than any other single mark of Spitfire. It was the main version of the fighter during 1941, replacing the Mk I and II in service. The Mk Vb was installed with the improved Merlin 45 engine, with two 20mm cannon and four machine guns mounted in the wings. A popular subject for modellers, the kit was of great quality for its day, featuring highly accurate outline and fine surface detail.

5 **1:72 Spitfire Mk Ia (1979)** Just as accurate as its Mk Vb predecessor but featuring the choice of traditional or snap-together assembly. Even in this relatively small scale Airfix's designers managed to capture the Spitfire's distinctive profile and elliptical wing superbly. It is perhaps testament to the strength of these simple but great little kits that both are still readily available today.

6 **1:48 Spitfire Mk Vb (1979)** This kit, together with its 1:72 siblings, remained the most accurate Spitfire kit British modellers could buy throughout the 1980s.

7 **1:48 Spitfire F22/24 (1996)** Along with the Seafire version below this was the first significant Airfix Spitfire release in over 15 years. The F22 & 24 were late-mark variants that represented perhaps the pinnacle of Spitfire development - now fitted with a redesigned wing, Rolls-Royce Griffon engine, cut-back rear fuselage and tear-drop canopy, more powerful electrical systems and enlarged tail surfaces. The F24, introduced into service in 1946, could reach a maximum speed of 454 mph, and an altitude of 30,000 ft in just eight minutes. Indeed, it was twice as heavy and more than twice as powerful as the Spitfire Mk I. Modellers were keen to build such an impressive machine, although some lamented that this 'super-Spit' seemed to have lost some of the graceful lines of the earlier versions.

8 **1:48 Seafire FR.46/47 (1996)** The first time Airfix had offered a Seafire kit, the naval variant of the Spitfire. The kit included options to build an aircraft with the wings folded (FR.47) or locked down (FR.46) and with flaps raised or lowered for both versions and front canopies for both aircraft.

9 **1:24 Spitfire Vb (2001)** Embracing the twenty-first century without forgetting their long heritage, Airfix released this modification of the 1:24 Mk I 1970 kit, containing additional sprues with a new prop, cannons and wing bulges, radiator and oil cooler parts, clipped wings, and various air filters to represent the 'desert' version.

10 **1:48 Spitfire Mk Vc/ Seafire IIIc (2002)** This kit was a modification of Airfix's 1:48 Spitfire Vb first issued in December 1979. It retained all the existing Spitfire Vb parts but also included four new sprues containing 44 parts for the Spitfire Vc and Seafire L.III.

11 **1:48 Spitfire Mk IXc/Mk XVIe (2006)** Airfix released their almost new Spitfire IXc/XVIe early in 2006. It comprised more than 70 parts, some of which were originally included in their Mk Vc kit dating from four years previously. A good offering that gave the option to build a popular mark of this famous aircraft in a larger scale than 1:72, but many modellers thought it not quite up to the standard of the preceding F.22 and FR.46 kits.

12 **1:72 Spitfire Mk Vc (2006)** A modification of the Airfix Mk Vb kit from 1974 which featured a new deeply scribed wing and two new cockpit canopies. Some inaccuracies of the 1970s' kit were also addressed to enable modellers to represent a fairly accurate Mk Vc – the first variant to be delivered overseas in large numbers, where it saw widespread service in North Africa, the Mediterranean and the Far East. This gave numerous options for interesting alternative paint and decal schemes.

13 **1:48 Spitfire Mk I (2007)** Airfix released an almost all-new kit with their 1:48 scale Spitfire Mk I, although it incorporated some elements of the 2006 Mk IX release. However, new parts included the entire fuselage, an all-new wing, and other specific details relating to early Merlin Spitfires. This kit gives the option to build either an early Mk I, a Battle of Britain Mk I or a Mk II.

14 **1:72 Spitfire Mk IXc (2008)** This was a completely new tool of the Mk IX, replacing the old 1960 vintage kit. Markings were provided for two aircraft: MK392 JE-J (the same markings but a different aircraft than the old JE-J kit). This represented Johnson's machine during D-Day operations, in which he commanded 127 Wing. The second option offered in the box was ZX-6, a Mk IX from Polish Flight 'C' No.145 Squadron RAF, the famous 'Skalski's Circus'. This particular aircraft was regularly flown by Stanislaw Skalski himself – the top Polish fighter ace of the Second World War.

15 **1:48 Spitfire Mk XVIe (2008)** This kit was only available to Airfix Club members. Packed in a Limited Edition box, it was a modification of the 2006 Airfix Spitfire Mk IXc, with a reworked fuselage (representing the later type with a cut-down rear fuselage and bubble canopy). Markings were provided for two very striking aircraft – a black and gold scheme from RAF 21 Group, and an aluminium and red-trimmed aircraft owned by Eddie Coventry of BAC Aviation.

16 **1:72 Spitfire PR XIX (2009)** A new tool of an interesting mark – the Griffon-engined high altitude photo-reconnaissance Spitfire. The kit comes with two decal options to represent either an RAF or a Swedish Air Force aircraft.

17 **1:72 Seafire Mk IIc (2009)** Another kit that was only available to Airfix Club members, this kit was part of a limited edition set produced to celebrate the centenary of naval aviation. The set also contained two other aircraft of the Fleet Air Arm – a Fairey Swordfish Mk IIc and a Grumman Wildcat Mk VI. The supplied decals represented Supermarine Seafire MB301, 8*D of 807 NAS FAA, HMS *Battler*, during Operation Avalanche at Salerno in 1943.

18 **1:24 BBMF Spitfire Mk Vb (2010)** A modification of the Airfix 1:24 Mk Vb kit, complete with decals to represent aircraft AB910 RF-D that currently flies with the Battle of Britain Memorial Flight. This machine (famous for its Donald Duck nose art) celebrates the plane of Polish ace Jan Zumbach, who fought in the Battle of Britain with 303 Squadron.

19 **1:48 Spitfire Mk XII (2010)** A new tool representing the Mk XII, which was the first production version of the Spitfire to use the Rolls-Royce Griffon engine. Its good low-level performance was useful in dealing with hit and run raids mounted by the Fw190, and later helped against the V-1, though the mark did not enter mass production. Only 100 were built, but despite this it is a variant that both modellers and Spitfire enthusiasts have been clamouring to build.

20 **1:48 Spitfire Mk Va (2010)** A special edition gift set that represents Douglas Bader's Mk Va W3185 'D-B', which he flew when commanding the Tangmere Wing in 1941. Released to promote the work of the Help for Heroes charity, 50p from every sale of this kit will be donated to the RAF Benevolent Fund, while an additional 50p will be paid in support of Help for Heroes.

21 **1:48 Seafire XVIIc (2010)** Another new tool representing an interim Seafire variant. The Mk XVII featured a reinforced wing and undercarriage, cut-down rear fuselage, redesigned teardrop canopy and an extra fuel tank. This kit will be appreciated by modellers who like to build aircraft of the Fleet Air Arm.

22 **1:72 Spitfire Mk Ia (2010)** Yet another new Spitfire tool, this time in 1:72 scale, of the classic Spitfire Mk Ia, intended to replace the Airfix kit that was released more than 30 years previously. The company's continuing focus on this famous aircraft, despite the fact that its first flight took place in 1936, is evidence of the sheer popularity of the Spitfire, its iconic status and the affection that it still inspires today. It is reassuring to know that as model kits are increasingly perceived to be a traditional toy, and even as many modellers become ever more demanding in their search for accuracy and detail, there still remains a place for the Spitfire in every tabletop airforce.

Tank firsts

Airfix's first tanks were the Panther, Sherman and Churchill, which appeared in the 1961 catalogue. However, the first real tank was 'Little Willie', built by the British in 1915. An improved version, known variously as 'Big Willie', 'the Wilson Machine' (after one of its co-inventors) and, most famously, 'Mother', went into mass production the following year. At 6 a.m. on Friday 15 September 1916, 'Mother' became the first tank to be used in action, at the Battle of Flers-Courcelette in the Somme. Not everyone was impressed – one aide-de-camp reportedly said: 'The idea that cavalry will be replaced by these iron coaches is absurd. It is little short of treasonous.' He was wrong, of course, and many of the cavalry regiments subsequently became tank regiments. Airfix released its first kit of 'Mother' in 1967, with two new versions following in 2009.

Right: Box art for the Airfix Chieftain tank, first released in 1971.
Below right: The WWI Male and Female tanks from the current Airfix range, with the latest CGI artwork and packaging style.
Below left: In the mid-1960s Airfix also released a set of ready-made vehicles in HO-00 scale, known as the 'Attack Force' range. This is the Patton tank.

WWI FEMAI

AIRFIX

1:76 WWI MALE TANK

K

Boom and bust

For Airfix, the 1960s was a period of constant innovation and improvement during which the company came to dominate the British industry in plastic scale model construction kits. The 1970s saw this domestic dominance extended to the international stage. In 1971 Airfix was awarded the Queen's Award to Industry for Outstanding Achievements in Exports, and in 1976 its international prominence was confirmed by winning America's Top Toy Trophy and a Gold Award for Merit at the Hobby Industry Show in Chicago. The decade was also marked by a series of acquisitions including Meccano, Dinky Toys and Tri-ang, and in 1975 Airfix announced record growth for the ninth year running, with sales hitting as many as 20,000,000 kits per year in 1976.

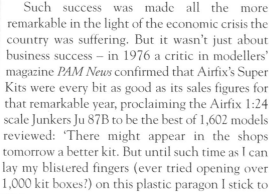

Such success was made all the more remarkable in the light of the economic crisis the country was suffering. But it wasn't just about business success – in 1976 a critic in modellers' magazine *PAM News* confirmed that Airfix's Super Kits were every bit as good as its sales figures for that remarkable year, proclaiming the Airfix 1:24 scale Junkers Ju 87B to be the best of 1,602 models reviewed: 'There might appear in the shops tomorrow a better kit. But until such time as I can lay my blistered fingers (ever tried opening over 1,000 kit boxes?) on this plastic paragon I stick to Airfix's admirable Ju 87B.'

The 1980s, though, was a different story. Whilst the quality of the kits remained impeccable, and the construction kits division continued to thrive, other parts of the group – including recent acquisitions Meccano and Dinky – were suffering. Exports were also down, all of which added up to disaster for the Airfix group as a whole. As Ralph Ehrmann later explained to Arthur Ward: 'We were terribly export oriented then... The pound went from $1.56 to $2.35 in a matter of about six or seven months and as a result our exports died. Customers did not want to pay 50 per cent more for the same goods as before.'

It was a simple equation and unfortunately there was only ever going to be one outcome. So the 1981 Earls Court Toy Fair, instead of being another triumphant platform for the launch of yet more superlative Airfix kits, became the scene of the announcement that Airfix had ceased trading. A long article in the *Financial Times* laid bare Airfix's woes: losses of more than £2m the previous financial year, the closure of the Meccano factory in Liverpool, unsuccessful attempts at financial reconstruction. But it was the quality of its products that would save Airfix, with Palitoy and Humbrol both bidding to buy the famous brand and continue producing Airfix kits.

In the end Palitoy won and Airfix moved home from south London to Palitoy's headquarters at Coalville in Leicestershire. But not for long. Within five years Palitoy itself was wound up, and in 1986 Humbrol succeeded in buying Airfix at the second attempt. Humbrol recognised that simply producing the best kits was not enough, acknowledging that the company must 'entice and excite new entrants to model making' (which it did by introducing kits such as the 1:16 scale Wallace & Gromit sets in 1999) as well as continuing to satisfy the core modelling fraternity, which it did admirably with hugely popular kits such as the 1:72 scale BAC TSR-2 in 2005. Humbrol also understood from the outset what a powerful force the internet would become in marketing and in communicating with Airfix aficionados around the world.

At Airfix's 50th anniversary, MD Frank Martin said that Humbrol would ensure that Airfix would continue to thrive into the new millennium. That much he achieved. He also said, 'Next stop the Airfix centenary.' That was a little over-optimistic – in 2006 Airfix was on the skids again.

Left and right: *Airfix Magazine* first appeared in June 1960 (left) with the subtitle 'Magazine for Plastic Modellers'. Three years later (above) circulation was still restricted to plastic modellers but by May 1981 (below) it was also being sold to human modellers. Despite Airfix's financial problems the monthly magazine was published regularly for 33 years, the last edition appearing in November 1993.

Dambusting Lancaster

The Christmas 1960 edition of *Airfix* Magazine carried an article describing how to adapt that year's Series 5 Lancaster kit into the dambusting version of the Lancaster, complete with bouncing bomb. The article pointed out that even in 1960 the bouncing bomb was still a military secret, and that the Lancasters used in the famous film had been vetted so that they did not bear too much resemblance to the real thing – all of which meant that the author of the article could only guess at the exact dimensions. However, the article explained, 'It is easy to get a cotton reel which is 1¼ inches in diameter, which is approximately the same size.' Inventor Barnes Wallis filed a patent for the bomb in 1942 but for security reasons this was not granted until 21 years later, in 1963, bringing the details into the public domain. Thirty years after that, in 1993, Airfix released its Avro Lancaster BIII Special Dambuster kit, which was converted from a 1980 Lancaster BIII mould.

Right (above): An original illustration from the 1960 article, showing the cotton-reel bouncing bomb.
Right (below): The Airfix Avro Lancaster B.I kit, first released in 1958.
Below: Impressive CGI artwork for the 2010 release of the Dambusters Lancaster. As well as a B.III special aircraft of the famous 617 squadron, this kit also includes a display stand and diorama base of the Möhne dam and lake.

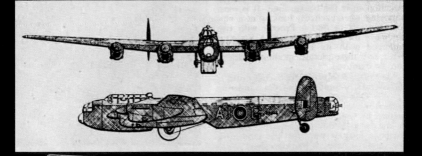

OVER
75
PARTS

AIRFIX

1/72nd **SCALE**
CONSTRUCTION KIT

AVRO
LANCASTER
BI

A Tooby

Hornby steams to the rescue

The demise of Airfix for the second time in 25 years produced a plethora of puns in the papers. The *Financial Times* went with 'Airfix Comes Unstuck…' and the *Observer* followed suit (going on to say the company's future 'rests on a scalpel-edge'), while the *Daily Telegraph* had Airfix coming to a 'sticky end': 'The engine is on fire, the nose is pointing straight down and, wouldn't you know it, the canopy is covered in glue: after 54 years Airfix was crashing and burning yesterday.'

When Hornby won the race to buy the ailing company the headline writers had another field day, *The Times* leading the way with: 'Hornby steams to the rescue of Airfix.' *The Guardian* followed up with the subtler headline: 'Hornby puts together deal for Airfix.' Again, the mantra for success was the same as in 1981, which was perhaps not surprising given that former Humbrol MD Frank Martin was now CEO of Hornby. The *Guardian* reported: 'The new owners will try to reinvigorate the Airfix business by investing in new products aimed at the younger market and also focussing on traditional products for older fans.'

Left: In 2007 Airfix introduced a 1:72 scale model of the all-weather RNLI Severn Class Lifeboat. This was available separately or as a gift set, which also included the Westland Sea King helicopter.
Above: Airfix's 1:24 scale De Havilland Mosquito NFII/FBVI, the famous 'wooden wonder'. It is the largest aircraft kit the company has produced to date, with a wingspan of just under 70cm, and features 617 individual parts.

And so it was: 2007 saw the introduction of the first *Dr Who* licensed kit, a new departure with a 1:72 scale RNLI Severn Class Lifeboat, a long-awaited Nimrod and a modification to the existing 1:48 scale Spitfire Mk I. The following year Hornby continued this momentum with no less than 13 new moulds: ten aircraft and three licensed character kits in addition to numerous modifications and re-releases. And so, on its 60th anniversary in 2009, Airfix was still going strong despite the ups and downs along the way. The name Airfix may have been coined as a reference to cheap, air-filled toys but the company has long-since evolved to fulfil the meaning that most people attach to the name: the very best in scale aircraft construction kits.

Right: In 2006, Hornby Hobbies relaunched the Airfix Club, a membership package which offered numerous benefits – one of which was an annual limited edition kit, available only to members. The 2007 kit was a 1:48 Spitfire Mk XVIe. It could be built into two striking aircraft in either black and gold or silver and red livery.

'10 things I wish I'd known when I was 10'

By Chris Ellis, former editor of *Airfix* magazine

From my point of view, I was luckier – if that is what you can call it – than most of today's young modellers, by being a schoolboy (well under 10) when World War II was at its height, so I saw and heard all types of warplane, Allied and German, around the clock. We all had spotter's books and read avidly the aircraft magazines of the day. And there was the bonus of 'Wings for Victory' weeks when real aircraft, usually war weary battle veterans, went on display to raise funds for new aircraft. The first aircraft I got really familiar with at one of these events was the Hawker Hurricane Mk I, where the officer in charge of the display – a veteran squadron-leader with an eye-patch – sat in the cockpit and explained all the controls and instruments to visitors who climbed steps on to a wooden platform rigged over the wing alongside the cockpit. I remember at the time being astonished by how big the aircraft seemed compared with seeing it in photographs and flying overhead. Later I made similar 'Wings for Victory' visits to a Spitfire Mk V and a Fairey Albacore biplane torpedo bomber, which was a good deal bigger than the fighters. I have many other memories of those days, of course, including an indoor display of crashed Luftwaffe aircraft, where the rather distinctive and sinister smell of the dope and fuel lingers in the mind to this day. These are just a few highlights from a continuous stream of events which fuelled our enthusiasm and excitement and there was always something new to see. I could, for example, show you exactly where I was standing on the way to school on the morning of 6 June 1944, when an RAF Mustang roared in from seawards, low over the town, and gave us the first glimpse of the distinctive black-and-white recognition stripes on its wings and fuselage, which had been applied to all Allied aircraft overnight for the D-Day invasion.

I mention all this because it leads directly to the first and most important of the '10 Things' – enthusiasm and knowledge of the subject.

Right: A Lancaster bomber on display in Trafalgar Square during the 'Wings for Victory' campaign in early 1943. This campaign gave the public a chance to see aircraft and other war materiel up close in an attempt to forge closer links between servicemen and people at home and – most importantly – to raise funds for the war effort.

THE SKY'S THE LIMIT
This is WINGS FOR VICTORY week

1 **Obviously, if you were not already interested in the excitement and drama of flight, and warplanes in particular, you would not be buying a model kit in the first place.** And it's also true that you could simply assemble the kit, paint it, stick on the transfers supplied, and put it on display. But you get much more out of any model hobby if you study the subject in connection with it. If you are already an aircraft enthusiast you won't need me to tell you this, but if you are a newcomer to the hobby start reading some relevant books and magazines. Try your local public library if your budget is limited and, of course, there are useful internet websites.

The Spitfire is a good model to start with and there are plenty of highly detailed publications on the aircraft, though this is true also of other significant types. There are several well-known feature films featuring Spitfires, too, but from a reference point of view the images are not always to be relied on, with such anomalies as the wrong mark, the wrong markings, and bogus squadron codes to confuse those not fully familiar with the subject. However, such films as *The First of the Few* and *Battle of Britain* are certainly good for conveying the historical context and atmosphere of the times, so they are still well worth seeing (and owning on DVD or video). But there are also some good documentary films, too, on important aircraft types and these give valuable detail and information for modellers. In the case of the Spitfire the most useful and interesting video I have is the Thorn-EMI Spitfire produced by Garry Pownall, which is superbly comprehensive and includes extracts from instructional films, all the key developments and actions, and ends with a pilot's-eye flight in a preserved Spitfire Mk IX. Get hold of this video and watch it, and I'd be surprised if you did not immediately want to rush out and buy a Spitfire kit!

As noted above, I'm just old enough to remember World War II aircraft in service, and that definitely made me a life-long aircraft enthusiast. But as is well-known, interest in World War II and the equipment of those days has never diminished, and succeeding generations are just as enthusiastic and knowledgeable as the old-timers. There are numerous museums – all the well-known ones – where you can see Spitfires on display really close-up, as well as all the other classic warplanes of past times. And there are numerous air displays each summer where, again, classic aircraft are shown, and flown. You can never know enough or see enough and even I keep coming across new information or new ideas. I go to the Goodwood Revival Meeting each year, mainly to see the historic cars, it's true, but there is always a fine air display as well with the chance to get up close to perfectly restored aircraft. About three years ago the full-size replica of the Spitfire prototype, K5054, was there, something I'd never seen before, and I don't remember the original either! I might mention here that my young grandson, who is the same age range now (5–8) that I was in late World War II, got to sit in the cockpit of a K5054 (and quite a few more aircraft since) and shows the same excitement and interest that I remember from his age. He has also made his first Spitfire kit from the Airfix range, got other Spitfire models, and his own copy of the Spitfire video. And he was born in the present century!

So you are never too young or too old to be an enthusiast, and aside from all the foregoing I suggest a scrapbook or ring binder to collect notes, photos, cuttings and so on to back up your interest and, indeed, a camera to take to air shows and museums and, maybe, even to photograph the models you make.

2 Get a proper tool kit together and keep it safe. This may sound obvious, but I've come across beginners who buy a kit – or are given one as a present – find they have no suitable tools and either break off the kit parts with their fingers or never make the model. For the average plastic aircraft kit you need the following: a craft knife with some spare blades, a razor-saw, pointed tweezers, two or three small files, including a round 'rat tail' one if possible, some emery boards, and some fine glasspaper. Additional useful items are an Archimedes drill with selection of fine drills, a small pencil or fine marker pen, and a small screwdriver or two. These extra pieces are most often needed

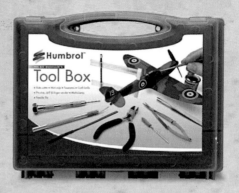

when you are more experienced. While modern kits are highly detailed, there are still older ones around where such details as pitot tubes or radio aerials, etc., need to be added, which is where the Archimedes drill comes in to drill the locating holes. If you come to do any conversion work later you may need to mark out cut lines and so on.

Complete sets of tools are sold in model shops, but all items noted here are available separately at model shops or from stalls at model shows, so you can make up your own choice of tools. Safety is important, so any purchased loose tools should be kept securely in a box. For many years I have used the traditional metal school geometry boxes, which are still sold in stationery shops today.

3 Build up a stock of necessary paints, brushes, and adhesives before you begin. Adhesives are most important for assembly work, of course, and most will be familiar with the tubes of polystyrene cement sold in all model shops. But even more important is liquid poly cement, sold in small bottles, sometimes with a brush built into the lid for application. Where this is not supplied, use a paint brush kept specially for liquid glue. In general, you can make a much neater job of assembly using liquid poly rather than tube cement. As a basic example, you just hold the parts to be joined correctly aligned and run a brush full of liquid cement along the join. Hold it for a few seconds longer and the job is done without any nasty blobs of cement being squeezed out along the join, as can easily happen with tube cement.

Tube cement still has its uses, though, such as cementing 'out of sight' pieces in place where the cement won't be seen, such as cockpit seats on brackets in the fuselage or undercarriage legs into sockets in the wheel wells.

Paint is a material you buy as you need for any given project. Some 'beginner' kits come with suitable paints for the model, plus a brush, which is handy to get you started. Paint is still available is 'plastic enamel', sold in tinlets and covering all the common camouflage colours needed for aircraft models, but the trend of recent years is to use acrylic paints. These are water soluble so brushes can be cleaned in water, making life easier for beginners and youngsters. Brush cleaner (white spirit) is needed to clean brushes used with plastic enamel. Most makes of model paints cover very well in just one coat, but, as with all model work, don't rush it and be prepared to apply a second coat where needed.

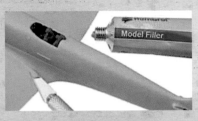

The other item that is useful to have is plastic filler. You might well need this later if you get round to more advanced conversion work, but it is useful, for example, on older kits, where you sometimes find unwanted 'dimples' or rough edges that need filling in. As with tools, keep all paints and adhesives, plus brushes, secure in a box and make sure all lids are tightly fitted so that the paint does not dry out.

4 Don't rush it. With the excitement of getting a new kit there is always an urge to get on with construction right away. But it is much better to take the time to familiarise yourself with the instruction sheet and relate the moulded kit parts to the diagrams. Very often there are sprue charts enabling small parts to be identified by number. Hence leave all the parts on the sprue until needed in the assembly sequence. Cutting all the bits from the sprue before you've looked at the instructions is a good way to lose key pieces and end up frustrated. It may be useful to check out reference books to find the actual subject of the model (if it's

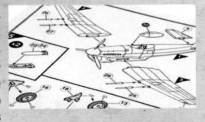

a well-known type) so you know exactly how the finished model should look. Most kits have a slip to return if parts are missing or poorly moulded. Checking out the kit first should enable you to spot any defects.

5 Paint as many small parts on the sprue as possible before you begin assembly. This makes painting much easier. Such parts as tyres, wheel hubs, undercarriage legs, dashboards, cockpit seats, bombs and rockets, crew figures, and so on are much easier to paint while you hold the sprue than trying to do it while holding a tiny part in tweezers. Any gap in the colouring that may arise from the small area where the part is attached to the sprue can be touched up after assembly.

6 Some kits have optional parts for two different versions. For example, a recent Airfix 1:48 scale Spitfire kit has parts enabling you to make it up as one of the first production Spitfire Mk Is with the first Spitfire squadron, No. 19, in 1938, or else a Battle of Britain version of 1940. Different props, different cockpit covers, and different markings are included. You need to make the right selection, of course, and I plan to make the 19 Sqn machine from this kit the next Spitfire model I make. With a bit of experience behind you, you can make detail changes yourself to simpler kits, such as cutting the cockpit and setting it in the 'open' position, or cutting out the ailerons and re-cementing them slightly 'drooped', and so on. Photographs of real aircraft, particularly in wartime, can show evidence of worn paintwork, exhaust staining, partly obliterated markings, repair patches, and much else. This is where your references come in, for a modeller with some experience can reflect this sort of thing in the finish of the model.

7 Take great care when cutting all parts from the sprue, file smooth the point where the part meets the sprue, clean off any moulding imperfections such as 'flash' along the edges of the part, and ensure all parts align correctly before cementing them together. Very young modellers need adult assistance here, but it is worth pointing out that there are some simple kits, ideal for youngsters, which largely 'click' together and don't really need any cutting or filing.

8 Keep a 'spares' box. Talk to any modeller of some experience and you will hear mention of the 'spares' box. In essence this is any suitable container where you keep all or any parts left over after the model is complete. This might be the optional parts not used in completing the Spitfire kit mentioned above, any unused crew figures, unused bombs, or whatever. Put any unused transfers from the kit in an envelope. Even the better pieces of sprue can be kept. In no time at all you start to build up a useful stock of spare parts that may come in useful – sometimes years later – for detailing or repairing other models. In other words, don't just ditch all the unused bits when you finish the kit. To the spares box you can also add oddments like wire, pins, plastic studs or anything that looks as if it could be useful for model detailing.

Related to this, most modellers of experience have a stock of card, plastic card, or plastic strip. This can be used later in conversion work, or possibly in scenic work if you set up a model on trestles for having its engine changed, to give just two examples.

9 If any model gets damaged by accident, repair it immediately. It is fatal to leave it for the proverbial 'rainy day', for by then the broken-off parts may well have 'disappeared' or the model has suffered more damage while resting unloved upon a shelf. If you have a well-stocked spares box, of course, you might find you can replace missing parts, but don't count on it!

10 Think about storage. Keeping lovingly made aircraft models neat, clean, and undamaged, and at the same time nicely displayed, is a major challenge in the hobby. Dust and damage are the enemy of models displayed on open shelves or bookcases. Hanging them on cotton from the ceiling is even worse. Don't even consider it. Years ago I bought a cheap four-shelf sliding-glass-door bookcase, added more shelves between the deeply spaced book shelves, and this holds over 100 1:72 scale model aircraft, safe and sound. For smaller scales such as 1:144 and 1:100, old shoe boxes make a safe storage, with tissue between the models. Obviously you can't display them in a shoe box, but the collection takes up minimal space that way. Larger scales, like 1:48, present more of a problem. If you have the room, the bookcase solution is fine, but my relatively few models to this scale I keep in the modern clip-top Useful Boxes, the clear plastic ones that stack.

Take your pick from these ideas, but, above all, have fun and good modelling!

People Power: The Airfix BAC TSR-2

The TSR-2 has become a cult aircraft, the subject of numerous myths and conspiracy theories. Initially developed in the early 1960s by the British Aircraft Corporation for the RAF, it was intended as a tactical strike and reconaissance aircraft, designed to perform the low-level, high-speed interdictor role. The type never entered service and numerous factors including political interference, poor management and spiralling costs meant that the project was ultimately abandoned. Indeed, only 10 test airframes were built, and only one ever flew (although two non-flying examples survive today, and are on static display in the UK). Contemporaries of the time saw this failure as symptomatic of the decline of British industry. Yet despite this it caught the imagination of many boys who dreamed of becoming fast jet pilots.

Some gradually forgot about this ill-fated aircraft, but for a certain breed of devoted modeller demand for a kit of the TSR-2 was omnipresent, and they were eager to build a plastic version of this peculiarly British aircraft. Following Hornby's takeover of Airfix, the company finally announced that 2006 would see a 1:72 BAC TSR2 – a brave decision, since demand was only expected to be about 7,000 kits. Airfix were worried, but ultimately bowed to pressure from its customers – a real example of 'people power' in action. In the event, the 1:72 kit, produced in limited quantities, quickly sold out and is now increasingly rare. It wasn't a perfect model by any means, but was a truly unique piece.

Perhaps spurred on by the success of the venture and the (largely) appreciative buyers, in 2008 Airfix released the TSR-2 kit again – this time in the larger 1:48 scale, with increased cockpit and interior details. It seems that if enough people request a specific kit, it might just get made.

Supersize Spitfire

When my 1:1 scale Airfix Spitfire emerged from Hangar One at RAF Cosford, pulled by the 26 schoolchildren who had assembled it, it looked magnificent. Gleaming in a brief burst of sunshine that cut through the rain, rolling slowly forward to the sound of an RAF band, it was a superb and emotional tribute to a great British icon, one of the world's greatest aircraft. Then the undercarriage nearly snapped off. But that was to be expected – after all, it may have been as big as a real Spitfire but it was still an Airfix model. And at least we didn't fill it with fireworks and blow it up, or shoot at it with giant air rifles, or launch it from the nearest bedroom window.

What I really liked about it was that whilst it looked like a Spitfire – it was the right size and shape, with some amazingly authentic details – it also managed to look like an Airfix model because the colours were a bit too garish, the transfers were a bit too bright, the tailplane was a bit too floppy and the wings were a bit too wobbly. And that's exactly what I wanted: not a replica Spitfire but a 1:1 scale Airfix Spitfire. It had all the signs of the unbridled enthusiasm I remember from my childhood: the way the paint had been slapped on and the pilot had been rammed too hard into his seat and the tailplanes were not quite level. I'm sure there was even glue smeared over the canopy.

Seeing that model come out of the hangar was a childhood dream fulfilled – I'd always wondered what it would be like to build a full size kit. It was also a world record: the first 1:1 scale aircraft construction kit made on the Airfix principle, and the biggest aircraft construction kit in the world by more than ten feet on the wingspan. It felt like a suitably epic way of celebrating the 60th anniversary of Airfix, to create a giant version of the company's most-tooled and most popular kit. Starting with the very

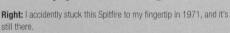

Right: I accidently stuck this Spitfire to my fingertip in 1971, and it's still there.

Above: A triumph for Thomas Telford School. The 26 schoolchildren who built the Spitfire pull the assembled kit out of the hangar. I'm in two places at once, sitting in the cockpit at the same time as directing operations on the tarmac.
Right: Error writ large. The code BTK was never used by a Spitfire squadron but it appeared on the first Airfix Spitfire, so to celebrate the 60th anniversary of Airfix we repeated the mistake.

first Airfix Spitfire in 1953 – the infamously inaccurate Spitfire BTK – Airfix has produced no less than 22 different versions of this legendary plane, including two highly detailed 1:48 scale kits in 1996 and three new tools to be released in 2010. Indeed, the Spitfire is so closely associated with Airfix that it appears on the covers of both the 50th and 60th anniversary Airfix histories and on the Airfix home page at www.airfix.com.

So what's the big deal? Why is it that nearly 75 years after its maiden flight the Spitfire remains probably the world's most famous aeroplane and by far the most popular Airfix kit? Why are we still transfixed by a plane that is chronologically closer to the Wright brothers than it is to the aircraft of today?

To find out just why the Spitfire has become so iconic I went to meet Carolyn Grace, who is the world's only current female Spitfire pilot. And while I was there I persuaded her to let me fulfil another childhood dream – I convinced her to let me fly a genuine Supermarine Spitfire.

Flight of fancy

Back in the 1930s, the Spitfire, along with the likes of Germany's Messerschmitt Bf109, heralded a new era of fighter design. In an age of fabric-covered biplanes with open cockpits and fixed undercarriages, here was a sleek monoplane with a metal stressed skin monocoque construction, an enclosed cockpit and a retractable undercarriage. It could fly higher and faster than anything before it (349 mph at 16,800 feet on its trials) and was armed with eight guns when all previous fighters had had two or maybe four. And that was just the Mk I – the final version, the Mk 24, was twice as powerful, had five times the firepower, a 25 per cent higher maximum speed and almost twice the rate of climb. To put this truly remarkable machine in context, it replaced a load of clunky old biplanes that were basically made out of bed linen and it remained in service with the RAF until June 1957, taking it well into the jet age.

It was of course an instrument of war – a machine for killing the enemy. But it was also a truly beautiful and outstanding piece of design and engineering. And the facts and figures only tell part of the story. It isn't until you've flown a Spitfire – or talked to someone who has flown

Below: This is an early Spitfire from the beginning of the war. By 1945 its power and armament had changed out of all proportion, but the essential shape remained as a tribute to Mitchell's genius.

one – that you really understand what's so special about it. Carolyn Grace, owner of ML407, a two-seater Mk IX, explained:

> The Spitfire appeals to all your senses. It sounds wonderful, it looks beautiful and it is superb to fly. The controls are in perfect harmony, and pilots knew it; during the war this was the machine they all wanted to fly. And of course it's British design at its very best. It's an icon that people really do find uplifting. I'm often booked to fly at funerals and I'm told that invariably when I make my third pass and finish with a climbing victory roll people cheer and clap, which is not what you expect at a funeral – the Spitfire just creates that good feeling among people.

It may be uplifting to watch but Carolyn told me it's even more so to fly.

> The designer, R.J. Mitchell, was undoubtedly one of the geniuses of our time. He designed the Spitfire to talk to you – if you're really working it hard it lets you know. It's not like other aeroplanes that will just flick out of a manoeuvre; it will tell you that you're just pulling a little bit too hard. With these amazing elliptical wings you can pull in a really tight turn and feel the stall buffet and you know that you're pushing it to the limit so you just ease off a little. And Spitfires were very good in battle because they were so well engineered that they could withstand an awful lot of shooting up.

Mitchell was dying of cancer while he was designing the Spitfire, and he knew that he had less time to live than the Air Ministry had given him to finish the plane. So he finished it ahead of schedule – the prototype made its maiden flight on 5 March 1936 and Mitchell died just over a year

Above: I flew a Supermarine Spitfire Mk IX. It was a Spitfire. I flew it. Have I said that?

later, in June 1937, at the age of 42. He didn't live to see his creation triumph in the Battle of Britain and he could not have dreamt that in 1996 some 80,000 people would turn out to watch a 60th anniversary flight of 13 surviving Spitfires take off from Eastleigh Airport (now Southampton Airport), scene of the Spitfire's maiden flight. However, he did live long enough to ridicule the name that Vickers (Supermarine's parent company) chose for his creation. Mitchell's response when he heard that his plane was to be known as the Spitfire was brief and to the point: 'It's just the sort of bloody silly name they would give it.'

Anyway – enough history. I wanted to find out for myself what Mitchell's Spitfire was like to fly. Carolyn took off with me in the back of ML407 and when we were airborne she gave me control. I was flying a Spitfire! I had dreamt of this since I was a boy. Half of my classmates would probably have chosen to play for Manchester United or something but the rest of us would have chosen to fly a Spitfire, every time. And here was I, actually doing it. It was an incredibly noisy, raw experience but I could feel straight away that this plane was something extraordinary. It felt alive. This was engineering from 70 years ago, worked out by blokes with pencils and slide rules and inspiration, so it was bound to feel a bit primitive. But it was fantastic. It felt like a living, breathing, roaring, panting machine wanting to do its job. Like a husky that wants to pull a sleigh. When we landed I was speechless. The camera was rolling but all I could do was laugh gleefully and say, 'This is a Supermarine Spitfire and I was flying it. I'm sorry. I can't say anything else. It's a Spitfire. *I flew it.* Have I said that?'

It really was something else. Now all I had to do was go and build one.

The 10 Airfix kits that every modeller should build:

1 **1:72 RAF Air Sea Rescue Launch** Released in 1979, this great little kit remains a modellers' favourite to this day. Relatively inexpensive, well moulded and with excellent detailing, the 63ft Type Two 'whaleback' HSL offers many opportunities for conversion or use in naval

dioramas. It also makes a good display alongside Airfix's and other manufacturers' ranges of 1:72 craft, notably the Vosper MTB and German E-boat. Operated throughout World War Two by the RAF Air Sea Rescue service, these boats and their crews, who lived by the famous motto 'the sea shall not have them', saved the lives of many downed airmen forced to ditch in coastal waters. The launches also played a part in early Commando raids on the French coast and the Channel Islands. The kit affords the opportunity to build either an early-war or later version (with added anti-shrapnel padding, machine guns and a 20mm Oerlikon cannon), with decals for three historical boats. Four crew figures are included.

2 **1:12 1930 Bentley 4.5L** A real Airfix gem, this kit was also available in 1:32 scale, which might be more suitable for less experienced modellers. The 1:12 'Blower' version is from 1970 and although hard to find, with patience and careful work it makes up into a beautiful model. The engine bay, for example, is superbly detailed and very accurate.

One of the most famous sports cars of the early 20th century, fifty-four Blower Bentleys were produced from 1929-1930. It had a 4.5L supercharged straight-four engine giving 175hp. The car raced at Le Mans and took the Brooklands Outer Circuit lap record to 137.96 mph in 1932. It's also the car that author Ian Fleming first gave to James Bond, in three early 007 novels – a true British classic.

3 **1:72 Martin B-26 Marauder** Again, an 'oldie but a goodie', this offering dates from 1973 but has been reissued numerous times since then. The kit has 146 parts – quite a lot for an aircraft in this scale – meaning that modellers can recreate a detailed interior, with complete cockpit and bomb bay areas. The bomb bay doors can be modelled in an open position, complete with 8 bombs. Two seated pilot figures and a seated mid-upper turret gunner are also provided. Decals are for three aircraft: 'Mild and Bitter' of the 450th BS USAAF, 'The Yankee Guerilla' of the 555th BS USAAF, and 'G' of No. 21 Sq. South African Air Force. The B-26 was a US twin-engined medium bomber. It was a challenging aircraft to fly, and several accidents following its introduction into service resulted in pilots nicknaming it 'the Widowmaker'. Nevertheless it was a key bombardment weapon for Allied forces and by the end of World War Two Marauders had flown more than 110,000 sorties, dropping around 150,000 tons of bombs.

4 **1:130 *Cutty Sark*** A large model (52cm in length) of 220 parts that demands skill and patience, particularly when rigging the vessel, but one that can make a terrific showpiece for a desk, shelf or display cabinet. A fine brush and a steady hand are essential! The kit is still being churned out today, despite the moulds being over forty years old and it is a great example of Airfix tackling fine subjects from the Age of Sail. Built in 1869, the *Cutty Sark* was a legendary Tea Clipper, plying the trade routes

between China and London. She could carry up to 32,000 square feet of sail, giving her a maximum speed of over 17 knots. In 1957 she was berthed in dry dock at Greenwich and has subsequently become a London icon and one of the world's best-known historic ships. She suffered extensive fire damage in 2007 and is currently undergoing restoration.

5 **1:32 Multipose Series: British Eighth Army** Famously commanded by Field Marshal Montgomery, the Eighth Army fought against Rommel's Afrika Korps and other German and Italian troops in Libya and Tunisia during World War Two. They are a good example of some of the celebrated and elite units available in Airfix's excellent range of 1:32 World War Two figures, which are great subjects to model and paint. They are ideal for use in dioramas or for playing with! The latest releases are moulded in plastic soft enough to be carefully bent into place to firmly grip the variety of weapons and equipment that are included with the set of figures. The figures come on sprucs in separate parts: head, upper torso, left and right arms, and legs. There are also accessories like pouches, packs, canteens, helmets and caps. A sturdy base is provided for each standing figure together with a small decal sheet including rank and unit insignia and complete painting instructions.

6 **1:24 Junkers Ju 87B Stuka** With 344 parts and a scale wingspan of just under 58cm, this is a serious model from Airfix's largest range of aircraft kits. The Stuka model has high quality engraved detail on all surfaces, with a complete Jumo engine and removable cowling, sliding canopy, spent ammo cans in rear compartment, separate wing brakes, navigation lights, removable wing panels, good cockpit detail (with pilot and gunner figures) and choices of 500 kg or 250 kg bombs to rain death on the enemy. A superb kit despite its vintage (Airfix introduced it in 1976), the Stuka

was the pre-eminent German dive-bomber of World War Two, easily recognisable due to its inverted gull wings and fixed spatted undercarriage. It was a potent ground-attack aircraft, becoming a symbol of Nazi Germany's early Blitzkrieg victories, but was also vulnerable to enemy fighters due to its poor aerial maneuverability, lack of speed and inadequate defensive armament.

7 **1:72 Supermarine Spitfire Mk Ia** This simple kit of a truly iconic aircraft is great fun, elegant looking and refreshingly uncomplicated. Nevertheless it is a modellers' favourite and builds into an accurate representation of the Mk Ia Spitfire, with good panel lines and fuselage, incorporating the aircraft's characteristic elliptical wing shape and gull profile. The kit is inexpensive, widely available and can also be found in Airfix's range of Starter Sets, which includes four acrylic paints, a paint brush and glue – ideal as a beginner's kit. It has much to recommend it and features in almost every Airfix enthusiast's collection – and as one of the most famous aircraft ever built, it fully justifies such popularity.

8 **1:600 HMS *Belfast*** This kit is widely considered to be one of Airfix's best in the popular small-scale ship range, featuring a high degree of detail and crisp moulding considering that it dates from 1973 (a vintage year in 1:600 scale, as Airfix also released HMS *Hood* and *Bismarck* kits). It is not without flaws, largely down to the limitations of plastic injection moulding in the early 1970s, but neverthless makes an excellent model with 250 parts. HMS *Belfast* was a Town Class light cruiser launched in 1938. She saw extensive service throughout World War Two, including actions at the Battle of the North Cape and during the Normandy landings. Decommissioned in 1963, she was designated a museum ship and is now preserved and anchored in the River Thames near Tower Bridge in London.

9 **1:48 English Electric Canberra B(I)8** A relatively new offering from Airfix in 2008, this model had been eagerly awaited by many modellers who clamoured for kits when it was released. Airfix currently produce four variants of the Canberra in this scale. It is a large kit containing 153 parts, decals for three aircraft and a 14-page instruction booklet. Sounds daunting? Not a bit of it. Modern high-quality moulding with good surface detail ensures that this kit makes an impressive model, but it is relatively simple to put together with logical parts breakdown and easy-to-follow instructions. Numerous options when it comes to ordnance also make this build lots of fun. The Canberra itself was a groundbreaking aircraft that set and held many altitude, distance and speed records in its early years. It was in service with the RAF from 1961 to 2006 – an incredible 55 years. The Canberra B(I)8 was designed for the interdiction role, and featured a revised teardrop 'fighter' style canopy for improved visibility, the ability to carry a wide range of ordnance, and an optional Boulton Paul gun pack with four 20mm cannon.

10 **1:144 Apollo Saturn V** This large kit dates from 1969, but was reissued in 2009 with nine newly-tooled parts, improving both accuracy and detail of the kit. It is a great build for anyone interested in the history of space flight, and makes an impressive and unusual finished model. The Saturn V was a multistage liquid-fuel expendable rocket used by NASA's Apollo and Skylab programs from 1967 until 1973.

Honourable mentions
Honourable mentions must also go to:

1:72 Sopwith Pup – a classic biplane in every sense.

1:72 DH Mosquito Mk XVIII – an excellent model of the famous 'wooden wonder'.

1:72 Hawker Hurricane Mk I – the aircraft that epitomised the spirit of the Battle of Britain.

1:72 Avro Vulcan – a great kit of the RAF's famous delta bomber.

1:72 Avro Lancaster B.I/III – a veteran kit from 1980 that still inspires great nostalgia.

1:48 Spitfire Mk Vb – a venerable Spit kit.

And also the fearsome Bengal Lancer from the superb 54mm range of figures.

A mouse the size of an elephant

Standard Airfix kits are made by injection moulding: by literally injecting molten plastic into a steel mould made up of two halves locked tightly together. When the plastic has cooled, the two halves of the mould are separated and all the components of the kit, interconnected by a sprue, are ejected from the mould. As a child I was aware of the basics of the injection-moulding process but I had no conception of the scale or speed of it. My dad worked in the steel industry so he knew a bit about tool making and I remember him explaining to me that the kit was made in a steel mould called a die, which in those days had to be made by hand. He told me that a die could cost as much as a house, and I remember wondering how it could cost as much as a house when an Airfix model only cost about 48 pence, because as a child I simply couldn't grasp the enormity of the mass-production process. In its heyday Airfix was churning out some 20 million kits a year, and that is a lot of kits – nearly 55,000 kits every day of the year, or 38 kits every minute of every day. It takes some of the romance out of that individual model you've saved up your pocket money for; that fantastic thing that you bought with your birthday money.

To make a complete kit using the injection-moulding process takes a matter of seconds but each piece of my bespoke 1:1 kit was going to be

Below: The first test piece from the quest for less weight. It was a bit floppy, but it was a start.

Right: This is an American P51 Mustang replica. Dave had to finish this one before starting on my Spitfire. That's the rule with Airfix.

individually moulded in fibreglass, which would take a matter of weeks. In fact, my Spitfire, which would be 72 times larger than the original BTK, was going to take several thousand times longer to mould.

But at least that would partly make up for the disappointment of discovering that each of my special childhood Airfix kits was only one of identical millions that had been spat off the end of a production line.

Timing was not going to be the only difference in producing a giant kit. There are certain problems that arise if you scale things up without modifying them – for instance, you can't scale a mouse up to be the size of an elephant because its legs would be too weak. That's because not all factors scale up proportionately: strength doesn't increase in direct proportion to weight, and so on. So creating the parts for the 1:1 Spitfire was going to be a very complex process, and to do that I called in a team of experts: Gateguards, a company that manufactures replica aircraft to order. Usually Gateguards build complete airframes for collectors, eccentrics, feature films or for use as 'gate guardians' at airfields, hence the name of the company. Their replicas are so convincing that one of the airfields they supplied had several letters from outraged members of the public saying how disgraceful it is to put a real Spitfire on a pole at the gate. But Gateguards had never made a construction kit, and that is a very different proposition.

Fibreglass gate guardians have been dubbed 'ultimate Airfix' planes but that is actually a misnomer because gate guardians aren't supplied in kit form. In fact, making a complete fibreglass airframe is so different from making a construction kit that Gateguards spent the best part of a week trying to talk me out of it. They said it wouldn't work because to build it as a kit meant there could be no structure inside the fuselage, no ribs, and no spars in the wings. That's fine for a 1:72 or even 1:24 scale polystyrene model but Gateguards said that to do that with a 1:1 scale fibreglass structure would be impossible: the model would collapse under its own weight when it was put together. They were right, of course, but – as we'll see later – a bit of emergency surgery during the construction of the kit soon solved that problem.

The other difficulty was that Gateguards had to remake their moulds so that the wings would split along the leading and tail edges like an Airfix kit – that is, so that the top and bottom halves of the wing would be separate pieces. The mould for a normal replica is split along the line of one of the spars near the centre of the wing, with the leading edge and the tail edge (the front and back of the wing) as separate pieces, which is much stronger and less vulnerable to the weather. On the plus side, using Gateguards' moulds meant that we were going to have something that a genuine Airfix kit wouldn't have. The original cast for the wings and fuselage had been made from a real Spitfire, so the panels of our kit would have ripples and bumps that aircraft pick up over years of use, including the knee indents just below cockpit where pilots had climbed in and out.

But there was one part of the kit that Gateguards weren't going to be able to make for me, and that was the pilot. As a child I always imagined that I was flying the plane that I'd just built. And given that this was my childhood fantasy I decided that the 1:1 plastic pilot in the kit should be made in my own image. As it turned out, that decision led to one of the most unpleasant experiences of my entire life.

Face/Off

We couldn't just stuff a shop mannequin into the pilot's seat: it had to be an accurate scale replica of a qualified pilot, so off I went to see Poppy Boden, who makes a living out of casting people's heads, hands, feet, bottoms, bodies and breasts. Now I'm quite claustrophobic – I can't even wear a full face motorbike helmet – so when she described what she was going to do alarm bells started ringing. She said that she was going to encase my entire head in plaster of Paris, except for two small holes near my nostrils. And I was going to have to sit there entombed in this Parisian iron maiden for 20 minutes, until it set.

In the end we settled for casting the back of my head first and then doing my face separately so that I wouldn't be completely encased, but even that was bad enough. First she told me to smile. Smile? The idea of being smothered for almost half an hour in a full-face helmet with no visor didn't make me feel like smiling. And anyway, I wanted my pilot to be steely eyed and combat-ready, just like the Airfix pilots of my youth. But Poppy told me a sombre expression would look lifeless and that I should look as if I was enjoying the flight. Well, it was a Spitfire that my doppelganger would be flying, so a smile was probably allowable…

Once I'd assumed the expression Poppy smeared my face with a warm blue gooey substance made from seaweed, which is designed to cling to the skin and pick up the tiniest of surface details – even individual hairs if you haven't shaved properly. That takes about three minutes to set and it peels off like Copydex. But it's very fragile and it would tear if she tried to remove it on its own so she then applied layer upon layer of plaster of

Left: We decided to cast the back of my head first and then do my face separately, so that I wouldn't be completely encased. Even that was bad enough.

Paris bandage until my head felt about four times as heavy as normal and looked – or so I'm told – like an Easter Island statue. Then the room went eerily quiet and I started to wonder if Poppy and the crew had gone off to the pub and left me. Eventually, after what seemed like aeons, Poppy started to remove the cast, which by that time was clinging to my face like the extraterrestrial in Alien. She was pulling and twisting and I was just starting to wonder whether my face was going to come off with it when we finally achieved separation and I found myself staring at a concave version of myself in intricate detail, right down to the smile lines – all right, wrinkles – round my eyes.

All in all, the face casting had been a deeply unpleasant experience but the worst was over. Casting the rest of my body was a relative cinch, especially as the pin that protrudes from the pilot's coccyx to hold him in his seat was going to be added afterwards: I didn't have to have that surgically attached prior to the casting.

Now that the kit and the pilot were in production I needed to recruit some Airfix enthusiasts to build it. I wanted young people, so I could find out whether they were as enthusiastic, committed and adept at Airfix as I was when I was a young person. A school was the obvious place to look, and there couldn't be a better school in which to recruit young modellers than one named after a great British engineer, albeit one who died before the age of flight – Thomas Telford.

Right: Steely eyed and combat ready? Or just worried about having his head encased in blue goo?

Thomas Telford engineers Airfix

The children of Thomas Telford School were great, but they're modern kids and they weren't that excited about the idea of Airfix. Maybe I was being a bit of a hopeless sentimentalist expecting them to be as excited about it as I had been when I was 13, because things have moved on. Life is different now. But I had to get them interested because they were the ones who were going to build the Spitfire. I had to get them Airfix enthused, and I thought I knew of a way. I got them all to build an Airfix tank and then I took them to Northamptonshire to compare their models with the real thing. And to drive the real thing. And to blow up their models with gunpowder. And to shoot at them with air rifles. Destroying your model is a vital Airfix rite of passage, and once they'd done that they were hooked.

And so to Hangar One at RAF Cosford, where the giant kit had been delivered by Gateguards and was now being watched over by a plastic effigy of myself in flying helmet and jacket, complete with protruding coccyx pin.

But now I was faced with my first big disappointment. The original plan had been to hang up all the parts on a giant sprue, like a proper Airfix kit, but that was going to require too much engineering so instead we had to cheat. We laid all the pieces out on the floor, arranged cardboard tubes round them to look like a sprue, and then taped everything together. We painted the tubes and the tape to match the blue fibreglass of the kit components and it actually looked very good when filmed from above but I was still disappointed that the pieces weren't attached properly. The first job for the children should have been to cut the components off the sprue with bolt cutters or an angle grinder or even a junior hacksaw, but the tape wasn't strong enough. The pieces came away so easily that it didn't really work. Having said that, once the components began to go together it really was like putting together a giant Airfix kit. While one group started assembling the wings and the undercarriage (using general-purpose silicon in a mastic gun rather than a tube of glue) another group started building the fuselage, which would eventually sit on top of the completed wing assembly.

At this point we discovered another of the problems associated with scaling a mouse up to the size of an elephant. A standard Airfix kit is

Above: After the insertion of a few scaled-up cocktail sticks the wings were self-supporting and the tailplanes didn't sag. Much. Then, just like I did as a kid, we marked out the camouflage scheme with a narrow line of brown paint. When we started filling it in with wide brushes the whole thing came to life very quickly.

moulded in polystyrene, which is a high grade thermoplastic that doesn't warp or twist, particularly when used at the small sizes of Airfix models. However, fibreglass is not so sturdy, especially when used for full size pieces that have been shorn of all internal support structures and transported from Cornwall to Shropshire on the back of a lorry. Just like the 1949 Airfix Ferguson tractor (which was moulded from acetate rather than polystyrene), some of the pieces had shrunk or twisted, so components that had fitted together perfectly in the Gateguards workshop now had to be coaxed into place.

In fact, this was just the sort of complication that had engaged me with Airfix as a child. I would spend ages trimming parts to get them to fit. I didn't just take it for granted that the two fuselage halves go together; I would try them, and maybe trim them for a better fit, or file down the edges and use a bit of filler to get a perfect joint. In our case, as Gateguards had predicted, there were huge gaps where the leading edges of the wings met but a few hours with an angle grinder and a jar of filler had that looking perfect.

However, it wasn't just the look of it – again, as predicted, the scaled-up wings were too weak to support themselves and the scaled-up tailplanes were too heavy to be attached to the sides of the tail assembly without sagging. If that had happened on a 1:72 scale model – which it wouldn't have done, but bear with me – we might have solved it by putting a cocktail stick through the tailplane and a lolly stick through the wings for extra support. So that's exactly what we did – after the surreptitious overnight insertion of a few scaled-up cocktail sticks (ie, box section steel tubes) the wings

were self-supporting and the tailplanes didn't sag. Much.

Then came the real test of whether our kit was going to work. It was time to lift the fuselage onto the wing assembly. With a 1:72 scale kit this is a fairly simple process. You just apply glue to both pieces, pick up the fuselage in one hand and the wing assembly in the other, and hold them together. But with a 1:1 scale kit you have to support the wing assembly on trestles in case the undercarriage gives way, lift the fuselage with a heavy duty engine hoist attached to a reinforced steel girder overhead, slide the hoist over the wing assembly and then lower the fuselage ever so carefully, listening to the creaks and groans of the wing assembly as you do so and desperately hoping that it doesn't all collapse in a heap of twisted fibreglass.

Remarkably, it didn't.

Even more remarkably, it was an almost perfect fit. And (with a little help from the trestles) it supported its own weight. A bit of filler round the joins and a little more surreptitious strengthening of the undercarriage with scaffolding tubes, and we were ready to paint our model.

Making an Airfix film

Nick Kennedy helped the kids from Thomas Telford School to make their Airfix film, using their 1:72 tanks as props. He explains how it was done:

When we started all we knew was that we were going to have two different types of tank – British Chieftains and Soviet T-62s – so the story was pretty open. You could retell part of a historic battle or recreate a sequence from a film, but in this case I just made up a little "ambush goes wrong" scenario. Watching a few classic war movies really helped to inspire us and gave us lots of ideas about exciting angles to recreate.

It is vital to storyboard the sequence no matter how rushed you are – each shot can take quite a long time to animate so we had to be sure that we got all the shots we needed. I drew out a cartoon strip-style version of the intended film, noting interesting scenes and camera angles. Tanks were a good choice of subject as vehicles on the ground are obviously the easiest to animate, although figures could also have been incorporated. We used about ten tanks in the end.

Next we needed to find a location – ideally something that looked like a miniature version of what we were aiming for. We were filming outside and found some piles of sandy mud that looked like small valleys and mountains and were perfect for the ambush. Unfortunately we didn't have any scale scenery but this would have made the backdrop look even more effective.

The great thing about making a film is that you can cheat a bit. When changing shots we moved the tanks for a more exciting backdrop, enabling us to shoot vehicles driving into the sunset, although we were careful to preserve continuity. Continuity simply means that the setting should look similar to the preceding scene so, when put together, the finished film seems believable.

We did run into some trouble in filming outdoors, because although it solves the problem of a realistic setting, filming outdoors requires consistent light. The sun kept disappearing behind clouds, which caused a few headaches. To take the stills we used a Digital SLR. This type of camera is ideal as it has full manual controls (exposure and focus are both really important) and the ability to use a remote trigger to keep the camera perfectly steady. We were also able to employ

a wide variety of lenses and consequently obtain more cinematic lens effects. A steady base or tripod proved to be vital too. We had a model that could be set up very low, which meant we could get right into the action for added drama.

Putting the stills together to make a stop-motion film was fairly straightforward. It can be done with any basic image animation program – we used Final Cut Pro. The first stage was to import all our images into the software. The program's automated 'import image sequence' function made this much quicker than it would have been to do it manually.

It got a little bit technical after that – I altered the default length of time that an image was displayed to between 1 and 2 frames per image. A normal film displays 24 still frames per second to convince the brain that you are seeing real motion. At a speed of 20 frames per second you will still get a decent quality image but below 15 frames per second the motion begins to look jerky. This consideration was key in deciding how many photos to take and how far to move each tank per image – i.e. if you are going to display 15 frames per second then you need to move a prop further in each image for the same apparent speed than if you were displaying 24 frames per second. A bit of maths is required, I'm afraid...

For example, if you want a tank to look like it is moving at 11 km/hour:

This equates to approximately 3 metres per second. Our film runs at 24 frames per second so that's 3/24; 0.125m or 12.5cm per frame. The tanks are 1:72 scale which results in 1.75 cm per frame. So for every frame in which we want a tank to move at 11km/h, we have to move it 1.75 cm between stills. Simple!

Once we had all the images in the video editing software we added a variety of special effects and music. Sound is vital in animations – as soon as you add in some creaky noises, exciting music, some machine-gun fire and explosions it all becomes much more engaging. I also spent a while adding in smoke and fire to add a bit of drama. We used real explosives to simulate battle damage but these were handled strictly by professionals only. Lighter fluid was also employed to capture the effects of a burning tank, and we also shot at the tanks with an air rifle to make some dirt splats. Please do not try any of this at home! With some ingenuity it would be possible to work something out without using

explosive equipment that would look similarly effective. The finished film was about 30 seconds long, but it took us 5 hours to plan out, 3 hours to film and about 10 hours of editing. It sounds like an awful lot of work, but seeing the end result on national television was worth it!

The most important advice I would offer to anyone who wanted to make their own film would be to keep every shot to at least 3 seconds (i.e. 72 still images) or the film becomes too confusing when you put it all together. Also, try to get as much material as possible when shooting – you can always cut the shorter sequences but it's almost impossible to go back and shoot more material.

An assistant is invaluable too. It's helpful if one person moves the models while the other can watch and check how it's all looking 'on set' through the camera. Practice and test it all first – before making the tank film with the Thomas Telford kids, I did one with some apples and potatoes in my front room just to see if my ideas were right about how far to move things in each frame. Finally, once you've set up your shot take a couple of tests to check you are happy and then be careful neither you nor anyone else moves the camera out of position – that's when the remote trigger mentioned earlier comes in handy.

Paint and decals – bringing BTK to life

This was the bit I was never any good at as a kid. I could never get the paint to go on evenly and I couldn't paint straight lines. Then of course there was the debate about whether or not to paint the parts before putting them together. My mate Cookie used to paint all the parts first, so he'd lay the wings and the fuselage out and paint the camouflage pattern on so that it would all line up when he put it together. Whereas I would paint some of the parts – the wheels and the engines and the insides of the cockpit and so on – but then paint the overall scheme on afterwards, which is how we did it at Cosford.

As a child I remember trying to recreate the camouflage pattern that was shown on the box. At first I made the curves in the lines between the green and the brown too gentle – they should actually be quite pronounced. And then I realised that they don't logically follow the surfaces of the plane; some of the brown patches went up the wing and then turned round and came back again with a patch of green underneath. It took me a long time to work that out, but when I started painting my planes like that they looked a lot better. I wanted the Thomas Telford kids to work all that out for themselves, so I took them to look at a few Spitfires and then we held a competition to design the camouflage scheme for our model. There was no fixed scheme for wartime camouflage patterns, so we didn't have to follow a rigid plan to make our model authentic.

The basic wartime colours of the 'temperate land' camouflage scheme were Dark Green (for anoraks, the nearest FS 595B match is 34079) and Dark Earth (30118), which were both introduced in 1936. Gateguards use a solvent-based paint closely matched to these colours but we had to find something that would be safe for schoolchildren to use, so we bought several litres of ordinary emulsion in roughly matching colours: Taragon Glory 1 for the green and Earth Glaze 1 for the brown. (They weren't quite right but that, too, was just like my childhood memory of Airfix – I never had enough pocket money to buy all the colours that might crop up so I just chose a green and a brown that were roughly right.) Then, just like I did as a kid, we carefully marked out the camouflage scheme with a narrow line of green paint, and when all 26 children started filling it in with wide brushes the whole thing came to life very quickly.

Above left: Once a dad, always a dad: James May Snr assists two of the Thomas Telford students with the correct application of the decals.
Above right: Various RAF roundels for the 1:1 Spitfire.

The crowning glory was the decals. We didn't need a giant saucer of water to soak them in because these were actually stickers rather than transfers. We'd chosen BTK, the erroneous lettering on the very first Airfix Spitfire, and we spent ages trying to decide where to place the letters and the roundel. Eventually, we decided it wasn't crucial because (as with the camouflage pattern) there was no standard placement – Spitfires would be delivered to the airfield with camouflage only and the numbers and roundels would be added at the airfield, which meant that each different squadron had its own variation in the size, colour and placing of its code numbers and roundels. One inaccuracy which we faithfully copied from the Airfix decals is the bright RAF red at the centre of the roundel – the red that was used for wartime roundels was painted with red oxide, which is much duller. However, we were not making a wartime replica, we were making a scaled-up Airfix model, and that inaccuracy was one of the things that made the finished article look like a model rather than an attempt at the real thing.

And so, finally, we were ready to reveal our model to the world – if the undercarriage survived the journey through the hangar doors and into the daylight. We didn't have any scaled-up cotton strong enough to hang it from the ceiling so, instead, the 26 children lined up with two ropes ready to haul it out of the hangar as the doors were opened. We fired up the smoke machine and I went outside to introduce the children and our model to the assembled gathering of veteran Spitfire pilots, fitters and engineers, Airfix artists, designers and historians, an Air Commodore, an

Spitfire parade

Some Spitfire colour schemes for the new Airfix model by **Peter G. Cooksley**

Mk I No 19 Sqdn. Duxford, August 1938
K9794. B Flt Scheme B. Upper roundels, type A1. Small serial numbers under wings. Wooden a/s. Also K9797. A Flt (red numeral) Scheme A.

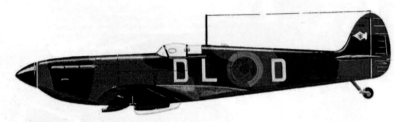

Mk I No 54 Sqdn. Hornchurch, May 1939
K9901, Scheme B. Upper roundels, type B. Black/white lower surfaces; colours divided down c/l. D/H a/s. Bulged hood. Sqdn badge on fin. Serial number repeated in reduced size on fin. Rim of former A1 roundel on fuselage overpainted.

Mk I No 611 (West Lancashire) Sqdn. Digby, Feb 1940
L1036, Scheme A. Upper roundels, type B. 3 ft diameter. Under wings only, black/white. Also 'D'. K9999 on fin (Scheme B). Under colours divided down c/l. Untapered radio mast. Port FY aft of roundel on both aircraft.

Mk I No 19 Sqdn. Duxford, July 1940
X4330, Scheme A. Upper roundels, type B. Lower, 3 ft diameter near tips. Also 'I' (with serifs) X4474 (Scheme A). Both a/c: Stbd QV forward of roundel and apparently VHF radio.

RAF band and an RAF guard of honour. Of course, it immediately started raining but that didn't dampen the sense of occasion.

> Ladies and gentlemen, thank you very much for coming to what one or two of you will still no doubt think of as No. 9 Maintenance Unit, RAF Cosford. We're here to witness the unveiling of the largest kit ever produced by the Airfix method… It has been built, as an Airfix model should be built, in a flurry of enthusiasm by young people. They are about to pull it out for you, and it's presented to you as a tribute to Airfix, to the joy that anybody has ever felt on holding a small Spitfire in the palm of their hand, to all the people who built, maintained and flew Spitfires and, most of all, to the Spitfire itself.

The band struck up, the hangar doors rolled open, and out of the smoke emerged my team of modelmakers hauling on their ropes. As the nose-cone emerged from the hangar the crowd broke into applause. Then the engine cowling and the leading edge of the wings emerged. Then the wheels lodged in the door runners and the whole thing ground to a halt. The children pulled harder and the undercarriage flexed. Was it going to collapse? Someone stepped forward to tell the children to stop pulling but before the instruction could be given the solid resin wheels bounced over the door runners and the model emerged into the afternoon in all its glory, the rain giving the wings and fuselage a dramatic sleek sheen.

Mission accomplished. There it stood, the world's first 1:1 scale Spitfire kit, and the world's biggest construction kit to be made on the Airfix principle. It looked superb. It was exactly as I'd hoped it would be. It was a childhood dream come true.

But it still couldn't quite match up to the realisation of my other childhood dream – actually flying the real thing. I flew a Supermarine Spitfire Mk IX. It was a Spitfire. I flew it. Have I said that?

Left: Camouflage and decal schemes for the Airfix Spitfire. There was no standard scheme for wartime camouflage or lettering so each squadron had its own idiosyncracies.
Right: There it stood, the world's first 1:1 scale Spitfire kit … a childhood dream come true. By this time we had tried to drag the Spitfire back into the hangar and the undercarriage had started to collapse, hence the trestles supporting the wings.

Airfix Spitfire PR.XIX: a step-by-step build

By Jonathan Mock

Most people will be familiar with the Spitfire through the Battle of Britain, but the aircraft also took part in a variety of other roles including unarmed Photographic Reconnaissance (PR). The Griffon-engined Spitfire PR.XIX was one of the later developments of this iconic aeroplane and was the subject of an all-new 1:72 Airfix kit in 2009.

Moulded in light grey and clear plastic, the kit has options for either RAF or Swedish versions of the ultimate PR Spitfire. The kit is easy to put together and the relatively simple colour schemes make it ideal for the beginner.

The first task is to remove the parts from the sprue. It is also worth checking the alignment of major parts (fuselage, wings etc.) at this stage to ensure a perfect fit. Any excess plastic can be carefully trimmed away using a sharp knife.

The kit includes a six part cockpit, which can be painted in a pale grey/green colour (Humbrol 78 is ideal), with the instrument panel and control grip in black and the seat in a brick red colour to depict the Bakelite plastic construction of the real thing. Dry brushing the parts in a paler shade of the basic colour helps enhance the moulded detail. A simple enhancement is to add seat straps using thin strips of masking tape – advanced modellers could order photo etched metal parts for this.

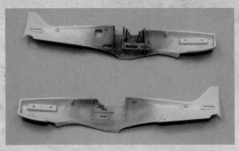

With the cockpit and fuselage interior painted, the parts can now be joined together. Liquid cement (actually a solvent) is best and is brushed over the join which then 'welds' the parts together. Strips of masking tape can be used to bind the parts as they dry, preferably overnight.

The kit wings are made up of three parts; the lower section is full-span and sets the correct dihedral angle. The two holes at the rear represent the vertical camera ports used for reconaissance. The centre of this section is painted in grey/green as it will be seen through the cockpit floor in the finished model.

A small amount of model filler may be required on the wing tips, which can be carefully applied to the gap and left to thoroughly dry overnight before being sanded down.

The wings and the fuselage can now be fixed together and the classic shape of the Spitfire starts to emerge. The parts are again left to thoroughly dry before cleaning up any joins.

In preparation for painting, the canopy is carefully masked using thin strips of tape before filling the rest with larger pieces. The canopy was later primed in grey/green to simulate the interior colour of the frames. The cockpit is also masked using tissue paper and a covering of a liquid masking agent (like Maskol).

The model can now be given a coat of grey primer. This not only helps in checking for any minor imperfections on the joins but also gives a better surface for the final colours. This can be brushed on using a neutral colour (Humbrol 64 is ideal) though many experienced modellers prefer to use aerosol cans. Humbrol make sprays specifically for this. When using spray cans apply light and even coats, and make sure you protect any adjacent surfaces with old newspaper. The spraying area must be well ventilated – a face mask is also essential.

While waiting for the primer to dry, some of the smaller parts can be painted. The propeller blades will need to be cleaned up and given a coat of yellow paint for the tips – yellow can be a translucent colour, so an initial coat of white underneath can

help here. The tips of the blades are then masked off and the blades painted black. When the masking is removed perfect propeller blades will be revealed.

The undercarriage parts can also be prepared. The gear doors will be the same as the underside colour so these can be left until final painting, while the main wheels and tail wheel are given a coat of silver for the hubs and dark grey for the tyres. This is more realistic than pure matt black. A good tip is to mount wheels on a cocktail stick and then rotate them around the paint brush to obtain a neat edge.

When the primer applied to the body of the Spitfire is dry and the aircraft has been checked for any blemishes, it is ready for painting. The final scheme can now be chosen – this Spitfire will be finished in the attractive two-tone scheme of Medium Sea Grey and PRU Blue worn by No.81 Squadron, Royal Air Force, operating from Malaysia in 1951.

The model was airbrushed Medium Sea Grey (Humbrol 165). This was thinned with white spirit and applied in light coats building up the colour, again using plenty of ventilation and a spray mask. Only the areas needing to be painted grey are airbrushed, along with the spinner, tail planes and canopy.

The paint was given 24 hours to dry before the areas needing to be protected – the upper surfaces of the wings and fuselage – were masked off using low-tack tape. The tip of the spinner was also masked while the tail planes were left off at this stage to make painting easier. The same masking techniques can also be used for hand-painting the model.

PRU Blue (Humbrol 230) was also applied in thin coats to the fuselage sides and undersides of the wings and tail planes, as well as the radiator parts, undercarriage and tail wheel doors.

After being left to dry for a few hours, the masking can be removed revealing neat demarcation lines between the colours. The model is again best left overnight to allow the paint to fully harden.

The rudder and tail planes can also be added at this stage - leaving the tail planes off saved a tricky masking job had they been glued in place. The rudder was offset slightly to add a touch of character to the model.

Weathering on this model was kept to a minimum and a study of photos will help in determining what and where to weather. For this Spitfire small dots of paint were applied to parts of the fuselage and wings and smoothed out along the direction of airflow using a flat soft brush moistened in thinner.

A wash of thinned paint was also flowed into the engraved panel lines around the ailerons and engines to simulate the collection of dirt and oil. Ground up artist's pastels were applied using an old paint brush to recreate the exhaust stain and the wear along the wing root from the boots of pilots and ground crew.

One distinctive feature of wear-and-tear on the Spitfire is the staining on the underside just aft of the carburettor intake. Black and brown paints were streaked along the surface using a flat brush. Most modellers prefer oil paints for weathering but water colours and acrylics can also be used.

Waterslide decals (or transfers) stick better to a glossy surface and help avoid the distinctive 'silvering' of the varnish surround which can happen if they are applied to matt paint. The model was given several coats of gloss varnish to help build up a smooth, shiny surface.

Once the varnish has dried the decals can be applied. Tweezers and a paint brush are best for positioning and applying them, especially many of the smaller decals found in kits. Some modellers like to use specialist products – like Humbrol's Decalfix

or Superset and Supersol – to help bed the decals down.

When the decals are dry (overnight is best), they can be sealed in place using a finishing coat of varnish. This model was airbrushed using a satin varnish to knock the glossy finish back, but still impart a 'scale' sheen suggesting a well-maintained aircraft.

With the varnish dry, the masking on the cockpit and canopy can be removed and the final parts added. The exhaust stack was painted a metallic black and dry brushed in dark brown to suggest heat discolouration. The canopy was attached using white glue, which dries

clear and also helps fill any minor gaps. The tiny tail wheel and doors were also carefully fixed in place using tweezers. The tyres were fixed to the undercarriage legs and the last step was to add the propeller.

The PR.XIX is a striking variant, perhaps the most attractive of all the Griffon-engined Spitfires and this kit makes a welcome addition to the range of variants available for modellers to build.

Complete catalogue of Airfix kit planes, trains, automobiles and ships by year

This list is restricted to new or converted/modified toolings only; note that kits of buildings, dioramas, accessories, figures and animals are not included in this catalogue.

1949
Ferguson Tractor (ready-assembled promotional item for Ferguson; not available to the public as a kit until several years later)

1952
Golden Hind

1953
Spitfire Mk I (BTK)

1954
Santa Maria
Shannon

1955
Cutty Sark
Southern Cross
1911 Rolls Royce
Spitfire Mk IX

1956
Gloster Gladiator Mk I
Bristol Fighter
Me Bf109
Hawker Hurricane IV RP
Golden Hind
HMS Victory
Westland Lysander
Westland S55
1911 Rolls Royce
1904 Darraq
1930 Bentley
1910 Model T Ford
1905 Rolls Royce

1957
SE 6B
Fokker DRI
Sopwith Camel
Albatross DV
JU-87B Stuka
DH Comet
DH Tiger Moth
RE8
Hawker Hart
Great Western
Santa Maria
Shannon
Cutty Sark
Mayflower
DH Mosquito FB VI
Walrus MK II
1907 Lanchester

1958
MiG-15
P-51D Mustang
FW-190D
Douglas Skyhawk
Auster Antarctic
Grumman Gosling
Revenge
Bristol Beaufighter
P-38J Lightning
Saunders Roe SR53
DH Heron
Wellington B111
Avro Lancaster B1
Westland Whirlwind
Fairey Swordfish II

1959
Hawker Sea Hawk
Fiat G91

Mitsubishi Zero
Hawker Typhoon
Jet Provost
HMS Cossack
Me Bf110D
Bristol Belvedere
Dornier Do 217
Fairey Rotodyne
1926 Morris Cowley
Travelling crane
HMS Victorious
Bristol Superfreighter
Short Sunderland

1960
Spitfire Mk IX (2nd mould)
Me 262
BP Defiant
Hovercraft SR-NI
Hawker Hunter
Bristol Bloodhound
Esso Tank Wagon
Blackburn/H-S Buccaneer
HMS Tiger
Railbus
Douglas Dakota
HMS Hood
Fokker Friendship

1961
Vickers Vanguard
HMS Daring
HMS Campbeltown
Panther Tank
Sherman Tank
Churchill Tank
Sunbeam Rapier
Austin Healey Sprite Mk I
Renault Dauphine

Morris Minor
Mineral Wagon
Brake Van
Cattle Wagon
Cement Wagon
Sud Aviation Caravelle
HMS *Nelson*
HP Halifax
SS *Canberra*
DH Comet 4B

1962

Stalin 3 tank
Avro Anson
NA Harvard II
Scammel Tank Transporter
1904 Mercedes
Meat Van
Refrigerated Van
Heinkel He III H20
Hawker P 1127
RMS *Queen Elizabeth*
Omnibus B Type
Boeing B17G Flying Fortress

1963

Yak-9D
EE Lightning
F-104 Starfighter
E Type Jaguar
Ariel Arrow Motorcycle
Lockheed Hudson III
HMS *Devonshire*
Lowmac
Scammel Scarab
Boeing Sea Knight
HMS *Warspite*
B-24J Liberator
SS *France*
Endeavour
Royal Sovereign

1964

Folland Gnat
Grumman Wildcat
Curtiss Kitty Hawk
15 ton Diesel Crane
Aichi D3 A1 Val
HMS *Hotspur*

Tiger Tank
German Armoured Car
Mirage IIIC
Il-2 Sturmovik
Vought F-4U Corsair
Centurion Tank
Volkswagen Beetle
MG 1100
Junkers Ju-88
HMS *Suffolk*
Prestwin Silo Wagon
Vickers VC-10
Scharnhorst
Mauretania
Catalina PBY-5A
1914 Dennis Fire Engine
Revenge

1965

Me Bf109 G
Bell Airacobra
Roland CII
CAC Boomerang
DUKW
Vertol 107-11
BAC III
Mitsubishi Dinah
Fairey Firefly
Buffalo & Jeep
Grumman Avenger TBM 3
HP42 Heracles
Boeing 727
HMS *Ajax*
LCM3 & Sherman Tank
B25 Mitchell
Junkers Ju52/3M
HMS *Victory*

1966

F5 Freedom Fighter
Westland Scout
M3 Half Track Personnel
   Carrier
Arado Ar-96
Thunderbolt
Westland HAR Mk I
Triumph TR4A
MGB
H-S Trident

HMS *Ark Royal*
Concorde
Old Bill Type Bus
Short Stirling
B-29 Superfortress
Trevithick Locomotive

1967

Fiat G50
Fieseler Storch
Avro 504K
Spad VII
Hannover CLIII
WWI Tank (Mother)
Vought Kingfisher
Douglas Dauntless
MiG-21 C
Airco DH4
Free Enterprise II
Aston Martin DB5
Porsche Carrera 6
1902 De Dietrich
Triumph Herald
Black Widow
Savoia-Marchetti SM79
Boeing 314 Clipper
Heinkel He-177
1804 Steam Loco
Cutty Sark
Wallis Autogyro

1968

Hawker Demon (conversion)
T-34 tank
Grumman Hellcat
Beagle Bassett
Angel Interceptor
Douglas Skyraider
Bristol Blenheim
Grumman Helldiver
Henschel Hs-129
Mercedes 280SL
Model T Ford 1912
Honda CB450
HS 125 Dominie
Grumman Duck
Fairey Battle
Petlyakov Pe-2
HMS *Fearless*

Ferrari 250LM
Ford Trimotor
Ilyushin Il-28
HP Hampden
Tirpitz
Handley Page 0/400
Queen Elizabeth II
James Bond Toyota
Prince
F-IIIA Aardvark

1969

Cessna
Lee Grant tank
Bronco OV-10A
Focke Wulf Fw-189
Douglas Devastator TBD-1
RAF Emergency Set
Ford Escort
Alfa Romeo 1933
Sikorsky Sea King
HP Jetstream
Lunar Module
Boeing 737
Jaguar 420
Ford 3 litre GT
BSA C15
BMW R69
Orion Space Craft
Boeing 747
Lockheed Hercules
Apollo Saturn V
Discovery
Hawker Harrier
SR-N4 Hovercraft

1970

DH Chipmunk
Bristol Bulldog
HMS *Leander*
Gloster Meteor
Henschel Hs 123 A-1
Leopard Tank
BAC Jaguar
Blohm & Voss BV-141
RAF Refuelling Set
Ford Capri
HMS *Iron Duke*
Russian Vostok

BHC SRN4
Supermarine Spitfire Mk I

1971

Saab Draken
Rommel
HMS Manxman
Chieftain Tank
Panzer IV Tank
Crusader Tank
Bond Bug 700E
Saab Viggen
DHC Beaver
Maxi BMC
Porsche 917
Vauxhall Prince Henry 1911
N American Vigilante
F-4 Phantom
Graf Spee
Douglas Invader
Lockheed Tristar
Saturn IB
Me Bf109 (1/24th)
1930 4½ litre Bentley (1/12th)

1972

Britten Norman Islander
Super Mystere B2
Morris Marina
Dornier Do -17
Monty's Humber
Wasa
P-51D Mustang (1/24th)
HMS *Amazon*

1973

Cessna Bird Dog
Gazelle SA 341
HMS *Hood*
Bismarck
Puma SA 330
DC-9
RAF Recovery Set
Maserati Indy
Martin B-26 Marauder
HMS *Belfast*
Moskva
Saint Louis
Hurricane Mk I (1/24th)

Dakota Gunship (Conversion)
Vosper MTB
Matilda Tank
Hurricane Mk IIB

1974

Cherokee Arrow II
Sopwith Pup
HMS *Cossack*
Chi Ha Tank
Scorpion Light Tank
Shooting Star
BAC Strikemaster
P-51D Mustang
Spitfire Mk Vb
German Reconnaissance Set
Republic Thunderstreak
BAC Canberra
Prinz Eugen
Harrier GRI

1975

SA Bulldog
NA Sabre
Narvik Class Destroyer
HMS *Ark Royal*
Bugatti 35D
Short Skyvan
Panavia Tornado
A300B Airbus
Rommel's Halftrack
Crusader III Tank
German E Boat

1976

HMS *Suffolk*
Fouga Magister
Me Bf109E
HA 5 22 Westland
Britten Norman Defender
  (conversion)
Army Lynx Helicopter
MG Magnette 1933
FIII E (conversion)
F14-A Tomcat
Concorde (update)
Junkers Ju-87B Stuka (1/24th)

1977
Me-163 Komet
Prinz Eugen (1/600)
Sepecat Jaguar
Navy Lynx Helicopter
Douglas Skyray
Henschel HS-126
Lee Tank (1/32nd)
Grant Tank (1/32nd)
Golden Hind
FW-190 A8/F8

1978
Whirlwind Mk I
P-51B Mustang
Star Cruiser
US Army Cargo Truck
Space Shuttle
USS *Forrestal*

1979
FW 190D
Spitfire Mk IA
MBB 105 Helicopter
Auster AOP6 (conversion)
Ju-87 Stuka
Boeing Sea Knight
Hawker Hurricane
Opel Blitz & Pak 40
Spitfire Mk Vb (1/48th)
Me Bf109F (1/48th)
Hawker Hurricane (1/48th)
Dassault Mirage F1C

Fokker Troopship (conversion)
S-3A Viking
F-15 Eagle
RAF Rescue Launch
HMS *Bounty*
Norton Motorcycle

1980
Douglas DC10
FW 190 A5 (1/24th)
MiG 23 Flogger
Alpha Jet
Hawker Fury (1/48th)
McDonnell F2H Banshee
Ford Cortina
Ford Zodiac
Ford Capri
Starcruiser Interceptor
DH Mosquito (1/48th)
Lancaster BIII
Ford C900
Countach LP500s
BMW MI
BMW Motorcycle

1981
Sikorsky HH 53C
Focke Wulf FW 190A
Christie Fire Engine (1/12th)
Shelby Cobra (1/16th)

1982
F-18A Hornet

F-16A Falcon
Sikorsky CH 53G Helicopter
Ju87 Stuka (1/48th)
HMS *George V*
HMS *Repulse*
Ford Express
Wild Breed Mustang
SR71 Blackbird
Burnout Firebird
Squad Rod Nova
Dragster
Black Belt Firebird
Night Stalker
Ford Mark VI
Chevrolet Cavalier
Sidewinder
Rolling Thunder
Saddle Tramp
Ground Shaker
Swamp Rat Jeep
Freedom Rider
Mount'n'Goat Jeep
Class Act
Sabre Vette
McLaren Mk 8D
Dust Devil
Bad Company
Thunder's Truck
Duke's Digger
Boss Hogg's Hauler
Cooter's Cruiser
General Lee Charger
Cooter's Tow Truck

Millennium Falcon™
Snow Speeder™
AT-AT™
Star Destroyer™
Flying Saucer

1983
X-Wing Fighter™
Hunter FGA 9 (conversion)
VC10 Refuelling (conversion)
Avro Vulcan B2
Kaman SH2 Seasprite
F5-E Tiger
A10 Thunderbolt
F 105 Thunderchief
Grumman Prowler
OV-10D Bronco (conversion)
Sea Harrier (1/48th)
Porsche 935
Ford Escort
Supercharged Dragster
Indy Pace Car
1983 Corvette
Toyota Supra
Fall Guy Truck™
Fall Guy Camaro™

1984
Kamov Ka-25 Hormone
Boeing 727-200 (Iberia
  conversion)
Rockwell B-1B
Lockheed U2B/D
Tornado GR1 (conversion)
Tie Interceptor™
Hughes AH-64 Apache
A-Wing Fighter™
B-Wing Fighter™
Hercules Gunship
  (conversion)
Tornado F2
Mil Mi-24 Hind
Sikorsky Sea King
Westland Sea King
  (conversion)
HP 0/400
Knight Rider™
Martin B-57B (conversion)

1985
Tornado F2 ADV
Hardcastle & McCormick
  Pick-up™
Hardcastle & McCormick
  Coyote™
Streethawk Car™
Streethawk Bike™

1986
No new toolings

1987
No new toolings

1988
BAe T45 Goshawk (tooled but
  not released)
Harrier GR-3 (1/48th)
Lightning F3 (conversion)

1989
Hawker-Siddeley Buccaneer
  S2B
Tornado F-3

1990
Short Tucano
Super Etendard
Mirage 2000
MiG Fulcrum two seater
Su 27A Flanker two seater
Hughes Apache (1/48th)

1991
Harrier GR5
Harrier GR7
Boeing AWACS E-3D Sentry
  (conversion)
Etendard (1/48th)
Ferrari 250 GTO (1/24th)
Triumph TR2 (1/24th)
Austin Healey Sprite (1/24th)
Jaguar XK-E (1/24th)
Jaguar E-Type (1/24th)
Mercedes 170 (1/24th)
Mercedes 500K (1/24th)
Alfa Romeo (1/24th)

Bugatti T50 (1/24th)

1992
YF-22 Lightning II
F-117A Stealth
Eurofighter EFA
Etendard IVP (1/48th)
Mirage 2000 (1/48th)
Tornado GR1A (1/48th)
MiG 17 (1/48th)
Scania Eurotruck (1/24th)
Refrigerated Trailer (1/24th)
Semi Trailer (1/24th)
Triumph TR-7 (1/24th)
Mercedes 300 SL (1/24th)
Bugatti EB 110 (1/24th)
Citroen 2CV (1/24th)
BMW M1 (1/24th)
3.5 CSL (1/24th)
Maserati Bora (1/24th)
Maserati Boomerang (1/24th)
Maserati Merak (1/24th)
Ferrari Rainbow (1/24th)
Ferrari Dino (1/24th)
Daytona (1/24th)
Lotus Esprit (1/24th)
Lamborghini Iota (1/24th)
Lamborghini Countach
  (1/24th)
Lamborghini Countach
  LP500S (1/24th)
De Tomaso Pantera (1/24th)
Corvette (1/24th)
Renault Alpine (1/24th)
Porsche 928 S4 (1/24th)
Peugeot 905

1993
Avro Lancaster BIII Special
  'Dambuster' (conversion)
HMS *Amazon*, *Leander* and
  Devonshire (all conversions)
F-15E Strike Eagle
  (conversion)

1994
Gloster Javelin FAW 9/9R
Sepecat Jaguar GR1A (1/48th)
HS Buccaneer S2B (1/48th)

1995

HS Buccaneer S2, S2C, S2D, SMK50 (1/48th)
Tornado GR1B (1/48th conversion)
DH Mosquito NF XIX/J30 (conversion)

1996

Supermarine Spitfire F22/24 (1/48th)
Supermarine Seafire FR46/47 (1/48th)

1997

No new toolings except for Airfix Junior 'Battle Zone'

1998

'Ships in Bottles' (tools from MB): *Mayflower*, *Cutty Sark*, Charles Morgan Whaler
Gulf Porsche 917 (1/32nd)
Ferrari 250 LM (1/32nd)
Vampire FB5
English Electric Lightning F-2A/F6 (1/48th)
English Electric Lightning F-1/F-1A/F-2/F-3 (1/48th)

1999

Wallace & Gromit Aeroplane
Wallace & Gromit Motorbike & Sidecar
B-17 Flying Fortress
Corsair F4U-1A (1/48th)
FW 190A-8 (1/48th)
P51-D Mustang (1/48th)
MiG 23 (1/144th)
F-20 Tiger Shark (1/144th)
General Dynamics F-16XL (1/144th)
F-4E Phantom II (1/144th)
MiG 21 (1/144th)
Fiat G91 Frecce Tricolori
Boeing 747-400 (1/300th)
Boeing 777 (1/300th)

Boeing AWACS Sentry
Eurofighter Typhoon

2000

BAe Harrier GR3 /AV-8A/AV-8S (1/24th)
Saab Viggen (1/144th)
F-104 Starfighter (1/144th)
Supermarine Spitfire Mk VIIIc (1/48th)
Grumman F6F-3 Hellcat (1/48th)
Curtiss Kittyhawk Mk Ia (1/48th)

2001

Westland Navy Lynx HMA8 (modification)
Lancaster BI Special (modification)
Supermarine Spitfire Mk Vb (1/24th modification)
Dornier Do 217 Mistel
CH-47 Chinook
Douglas DC3 Dakota
C130 Hercules
Toyota Rav 4 (1/24th)
MGB (1/24th)
Aston Martin DB5 (1/24th)
McLaren F1 (1/43rd)
Williams F1 (1/43rd)
Citroen Xsara T4 WRC (1/43rd)
Subaru Impreza (1/43rd)
Peugeot 206 WRC (1/43rd)
Citroen Xsara T4 WRC (1/24th)
Peugeot 206 WRC (1/24th)

2002

Spitfire Mk Vc/Seafire IIIc (1/48th modification)
BAe Sea Harrier FRS-1 (1/24th modification)
Saab JA-37 Viggen (1/48th)
Sepecat Jaguar GR3 (1/48th)
Dassault Super Etendard (1/48th)
Ford Focus (1/43rd)

Mitsubishi WRC (1/43rd)
Mitsubishi WRC (1/24th)
Subaru Impreza WRC (1/24th)
Honda 500cc (1/24th)
Suzuki 500cc (1/24th)
Yamaha 500cc (1/24th)

2003

BAe Red Arrows Hawk (1/48th)
BAe Hawk 100 Series (1/48th)
DH Mosquito NF 30 (1/48th modification)
DH Mosquito B Mk XVI/PR XVI (1/48th modification)
NA F-86F Sabre
Subaru Ev2 Asphalt (1/43rd)
Ford Focus WRC (1/24th)
Peugeot 206 WRC Safari (1/24th)
Honda 4-stroke (1/24th)
Honda 500cc NSR500 (1/24th)
Yamaha 500cc Y2RM1 (1/24th)

2004

Panavia Tornado GR4/4A
Panavia Tornado F3/EF3 (1/48th)
Boeing AH-64D Apache Longbow
Bell AH-1T Sea Cobra
Challenger II Tank (1/35th)
Abrams M1A2 Tank (1/35th)
GMC DUKW (1/35th)
Sukhoi Su-27 Flanker B
Concorde
LCVP Landing Craft
Willys Jeep
GMC Truck

2005

BAC TSR-2
Supermarine Spitfire Mk IX/Mk XVIe (1/48th)
Supermarine Spitfire Mk Vc (modification)
NA P-51K Mustang (1/24th modification)
Sherman 'Crab' Tank (1/76th)

Churchill 'Crocodile' Tank
(1/76th)
NA T-6G Texan
Saab S/J-29 Tunnan

2006
Wallace & Gromit Anti-Pesto
Van (1/12th)
Britten Norman Islander
(modification)
DH Drago Rapide
Lockheed Super Constellation
HMS *Hood* (1/400th)
HMS *King George V* (1/400th)
Scharnhorst & Gneisenau
(1/400th)
Bismarck & Tirpitz (1/400th)

2007
HS Nimrod MR-2P
RNLI Severn Class Lifeboat
Dr Who 'Welcome Aboard'
Supermarine Spitfire Mk I
(1/48th modification)

2008
BAe Red Arrows Hawk
Supermarine Spitfire Mk IXc
BAe Hawk 128/132
EE Canberra B(I)8
EE Canberra PR 9
EE Canberra B2/B20 (1/48th)
EE Canberra B(I)8 (1/48th)
EE Canberra PR 9 (1/48th)
BAC TSR-2 (1/48th)
Shaun the Sheep with Land
Rover (1/48th)
Shaun the Sheep with Tractor
(1/48th)
Fairey Fulmar Mk I/II
Hawker Sea Fury
Hawker Tempest V
Gloster Meteor F8
Boeing AH-64 Apache
Longbow
Boeing Chinook
Horsa Glider
Vickers Wellington Mk IA/IC
Focke Wulf Mistel

HMS *Montgomery* (1/400th)
HNoMS *St Albans* (1/400th)
Gloster Gladiator
(modification)
HS Buccaneer RAF & Navy
(modification)
Fokker F27 Friendship
(modification)
Supermarine Spitfire Mk XVIe
(modification)
Sherman 'Calliope' Tank
Matilda 'Hedgehog'
Churchill Bridge Layer
Airfix also released 12 former
JB models of 1/76th scale
military vehicles.

2009
De Havilland Mosquito NF
II/FB VI (1/24th)
Yakovlev Yak 9D
Bell P-39Q Airacobra
Grumman Widgeon/Gosling
Hannover CL111
RE8
Albatross D.Va
Bristol Fighter F2B
Supermarine Walrus Mk II
Ilyushin Sturmovik
Spitfire PR XIX
Messerschmitt BF-109 G
Curtiss SB2C Helldiver
Vought F4U Corsair (FAA)
Blohm & Voss Bv141
Petlyakov Pe2
Focke Wulf FW189
HS Sea Vixen FAW2 (1/48th)

Sea Harrier FRS1 (new tool)
Sea Harrier FA2 (new tool)
Hawker Hurricane MkIIc (new
tool)
MiG 15 (new tool)
HMS *Warspite* (1/600th)
HMS *Iron Duke* (1/600th)
HMS *Illustrious* (1/350th)
Titanic (1/700th)
Golden Hind (1/72nd)
WWI Male Tank
WWI Female Tank
(modification)
DUKW
F-18 Hornet (1/111th new tool)
Hughes AH-64 Apache
(1/144th new tool)
Vulcan XH558
BBMF Spitfire Mk Vb
Apollo Saturn V
(modification)
Lunar Module
Airfix also released 20 'Starter
Kits' of simplified aircraft
and cars

2010
Spitfire Mk1a (new tool)
Messerschmitt Bf110 C/D
(new tool)
Messerschmitt Bf110 E (new
tool)
North American F-86F Sabre
(new tool)
Canadair Mk.4 Sabre (new
tool)
BAe Hawk T1 (new tool)

BAe Harrier GR9 (new tool)
Spitfire MkXII (1/48th new
    tool)
Messerschmitt Bf109E (1/48th
    new tool)
Messerschmitt Bf109E Tropical
    (1/48th new tool)
Seafire XVIIc (1/48th new
    tool)
Westland Lynx - Navy HMA8
    / Super Lynx (1/48th new
    tool)
Westland Lynx - Army AM-7
    (1/48th new tool)
Trafalgar class submarine
    (1/350th new tool)

Jaguar XKRGT3 APEX Racing
    (1/32nd new tool)
Aston Martin DBR9 Gulf
    (1/32nd new tool)
Bedford QL Trucks – QLT &
    QLD (1/76th new tool)
Vickers Valiant (1/72nd new
    tool)
BTK Spitfire (1/72nd)
Comet Racer (1/72nd)
Spitfire MkVb (1/72nd)
Messerchmitt Bf109E (1/72nd)
Hawker Hurricane Mk1
    (1/72nd)
Junkers Ju88 (1/72nd)
Junkers Ju87-B (1/72nd)

Fairey Battle
Handley Page Hampden
    (1/72nd)
Boeing 737 (1/144th)
Boeing 727 (1/144th)
Heinkel HeIII (1/72nd)
B-24 Liberator (1/72nd)
Junkers Ju87-B Stuka (1/48th)
Bae Hawk T1 (1/48th)
BAe Harrier GR3 (1/24th)
Vostok 1 (1/144th)
Saturn 1B (1/144th)
Saturn V Skylab (1/144th)
Supermarine Spitfire MkVa
    (Douglas Bader, 1/48th)

Useful websites

Official Airfix Club **http://www.airfix.com/official-airfix-club-membership**
Airfix Clubs directory **http://www.airfix.com/clubs-directory**
Airfix Collectors' Club **http://pws.prserv.net/gbinet.dbjames/acc.htm**
Online community for collecting enthusiasts, with contributions from Airfix historian
Arthur Ward: **http://collectingfriends.com/content**
International Plastic Modelling Society **http://www.ipms-uk.co.uk**